My wife and I decided to get scuba certified for our twenty-fifth wedding anniversary. It was just one of those bucket list things we'd always wanted to do—to renew our vows on the bottom of the ocean. We did this using only sign language, of course. Picture thumbs up for "better" and thumbs down for "worse," and you'll get the idea. The actual art of scuba is mostly about learning to breathe with a mask on. First-timers suddenly realize they are actually under water, and their natural tendency is to start breathing too fast. In golf, the number one rule is to keep your head down. In baseball, it's to keep your eye on the ball. In scuba diving, it's just breathe. Keith's book brings that scuba diving lesson to dry land. His story seems like something a screenwriter wouldn't even try to write. It's one chapter after another of a life's downward spiral. But somehow through it all, he was able to keep breathing. He's a walking miracle in many ways, but the first rule of scuba will always ring true for him: just breathe. My hope is that you will see parts of yourself in Keith's story and realize that none of us live too far away from the grace of God. I hope you will see addiction for the monster that it is and seek some help before it is too late for you. So read on. Keep your mask on. Don't freak out. Just breathe. And discover the hope you need.

—**Tim Harlow,** *senior pastor, Parkview Christian Church, Orland Park, Illinois; the author of* Life on Mission

Sometimes "amazing grace" seems like just a phrase or only the title of an old hymn. And then you read the story of a life like Keith's, and it becomes clear once again that this grace is a power stronger than death and it's the hope of the world. Read about it—and come home.

—**John Ortberg,** *senior pastor, Menlo Park Presbyterian Church, CA*

Just Breathe is the riveting depiction of a remarkably transformed life. Keith's journey reveals one of the most powerful stories of redemption I have ever witnessed in over thirty-five years of pastoring.

—**Pastor Jude Fouquier,** *lead pastor,*
The City Church, Ventura, CA

Ever wondered if God does miracles? Ever wondered if He can do miracles today, perhaps in your life? With *Just Breathe,* you hold in your hands the story of a real-life modern miracle. Keith's story can be your story and reminds us that none of us are beyond hope.

—**Gene Appel,** *senior pastor, Eastside Christian Church,*
Anaheim, CA

Watching God transform Keith and his family has been one of the greatest privileges of my life! If you feel like you are buried under shame, that you're *too far gone* or that you could never get beyond your past, this book is for you. There is hope for you! Keith's story continues to be a vivid reminder to me that Jesus doesn't just make us better—He makes us new!

—**Jodi Hickerson,** *programming director,*
Mission Church, Ventura, CA

If you feel like you've somehow outrun God's grace, think again. Keith's story about his journey to freedom is proof that God will go to any lengths to save anybody, including you.

—**Mike Foster,** *founder of People of the Second Chance;*
creator of the Rescue Academy; author of People of
the Second Chance *and* Freeway

JUST BREATHE

All stories redeemable

All brokenness reparable

All addictions breakable

KEITH REPULT

WITH MIKE BREAUX AND JEN OAKES

BroadStreet
PUBLISHING

BroadStreet Publishing® Group, LLC
Racine, Wisconsin, USA
BroadStreetPublishing.com

JUST BREATHE
All Stories Redeemable, All Brokenness Reparable, All Addictions Breakable

ISBN-13: 978-1-4245-5520-8 (softcover)
ISBN-13: 978-1-4245-5521-5 (e-book)

Stock or custom editions of BroadStreet Publishing titles may be purchased in bulk for educational, business, ministry, fundraising, or sales promotional use. For information, please e-mail info@ broadstreetpublishing.com.

Cover design by Garborg Design
Interior design and typesetting by Katherine Lloyd | theDESKonline.com.

Printed in the United States of America
17 18 19 20 21 5 4 3 2 1

For Drew

CONTENTS

Part One: *The Journey*

Part Two: *The Tools*

FOREWORD

By George Barna

Life is not easy. If you have any doubt, read *Just Breathe*, the narrative of Keith Repult's life. It is a story of one man's struggle to overcome physical abuse, abandonment, homelessness, sexual promiscuity, loneliness, deceit, manipulation, regret, addiction, and the loss of hope. As you read his story, you will marvel that he lived through it all. And at times you may wonder why he bothered to keep going. At points in the story, you may conclude that his was an irredeemable, unsalvageable life.

But in God's eyes there is no such thing as a life that is irredeemable or unsalvageable. Keith eventually hit rock bottom—several times—and at one juncture decided to take a chance on God and invite Him to intervene. From that point forward, Keith's life transitioned to a tale of forgiveness, restoration, hope, healing, purpose, and even joy. There were bumps and bruises along the way, even after God became a vital part of Keith's daily experience, but the trajectory was totally altered.

This is the kind of life story you might expect from Hollywood—you know, the "based on a true story" bio-pic that is usually more "based on" than "true story." But Keith's story is not a fabricated, dressed up Hollywood drama. It is a heartwarming chronicle about the courage of a man and the love of his Creator. It is a transparent account of how God once again proves that He loves all people, even those who spend a few decades denying, offending, and ignoring Him.

Having spent several years researching how God transforms peoples' lives, a process recapped in my book *Maximum Faith*, Keith's story fits the pattern that the research discovered. Everyone is on a spiritual journey, and there are ten stops on that journey. Because God has given us free will, we don't have to go any farther on that journey than we want to. Most people never get beyond stop three (believing that God exists, but not engaging Him in a life-altering relationship). Most "devoted" Christians never get past stop five (having a relationship with God through Jesus Christ, and being active in a church, but never truly living for and like Jesus).

Keith, however, gave God the license to break and then heal him. That willingness to accept brokenness and then the restoration that God always wants to provide are what have enabled his life to become a significantly transformed one. God invariably seeks to break us from our love of sin, self, and society. He does it to glorify Himself, yes, but to also benefit us beyond measure. For that process to work, though, we have to accept brokenness as an irrefutable part of our spiritual growth process.

Sadly, my research showed that almost all born-again Christians have had multiple opportunities to experience and accept brokenness through specific crises God allowed in their life, but our typical reaction is to fend off those opportunities by either seeking to avoid brokenness or by striving to heal ourselves. We reject brokenness as if it is a mark of weakness or being a loser—unfortunate perspectives our secular society is eager to advance.

(Surprisingly, the research also revealed that churches are usually complicit in rejecting the benefits of brokenness, devoting more effort into keeping congregants happy and connected than to facilitating their wholeness.)

When we embrace brokenness as a gift rather than as a curse, God is able to come alongside us and lead us to the next stop on the journey: surrender and submission. Incorporating surrender to God's control and principles—and submitting to His authority and His agenda—gives our lives deeper meaning and focus. It moves us closer to becoming people for whom our love of God and love of people are evident in everything we think, say, and do.

Because he is fully human, I know Keith will never live a perfect life. But because he has embraced God's gift of brokenness and is an active participant in surrendering and submitting his life to God, he is maximizing his spiritual and life potential. His story is yet another shred of proof that God is alive and at work in people's lives, restoring us to Himself in ways we would not choose and perhaps cannot imagine, using processes we cannot orchestrate or control, and glorifying Himself through broken but willing vessels like Keith.

Read the pages that follow. Keith's life was a mess. God redeemed him and now his life is an imperfect but beautiful testimony to the love of God and how He blesses those whom He restores. In the classic hymn "Amazing Grace," Anglican minister John Newton wrote of his own experience with brokenness and God's subsequent rescue: "I once was lost, but now am found; was blind, but now I see." That could well be the theme song for Keith's story.

George Barna, *New York Times* best-selling author
Ventura, CA
April 2017

INTRODUCTION

By Mike Breaux

My favorite flavor is the key lime pie, or maybe the oatmeal raisin cookie. You can find them in a great little frozen yogurt shop in Ventura, California. Ventura is a funky beach town with a really cool vibe. Thrift stores. Surfer dudes. Former Hell's Angels bikers. Endless strawberry fields and orange groves. Lots of retro and reclaimed décor. And lots of reclaimed lives. My buddy Keith, in particular.

He came to Ventura to open the yogurt shop, but he really came to hide. Hide from his past. Hide from his reputation. Hide from his shame. Hide from himself. Hide from God. Try as we might, though, hiding from any of that is really futile ... especially the God part. Not only does God know everything about us, but he also relentlessly pursues us with an unfailing love. In fact, he'd been pursuing Keith for a long time.

I remember the day Keith called me to say how he was so proud to be asked to come to his son's elementary class on Career Day. It's that day when parents get up and talk about what they do for a living. I've stood there before knowing that I was going to have to follow the fighter pilot, football player, or firefighter.

It can be pretty intimidating. When it was Keith's turn, he passed out various flavors of fro-yo along with the kids' favorite toppings. He was the absolute hit of the day. Take that you brave, cool astronauts!

It was the first time he was able to stand in front of people and proudly tell them what he did for a career. It was a freeing moment and one he thought he might never experience. Keith and I jokingly refer to his journey as one from hard core to soft serve. For years he had risen to the top of the adult entertainment industry, distributing porn with the rationalization that it was no different than passing out frozen yogurt samples.

But you know that rationalize really means "rational-lies," right? Keith felt all kinds of guilt about his life. And eventually that guilt morphed into shame. You see, you feel guilt for something you did. You feel shame for someone you are. And he didn't like who he had become.

Keith surrendered his life to Jesus Christ about five years ago. Shame is the language of the thief, but grace is the language of Jesus. That shame was replaced with unconditional love, a love that met him right where he was ... as he was. As a friend assured him, "God knew what he got when he got you."

It has been an honor to walk with Keith on this journey. To have a front row seat to his transformation has been one of the highlights of my life. I have had the honor of helping him keep track of days clean, helping him recover from relapse, and trying to answer his questions about life and God. Allowing him to teach me afresh about the grace of God has been such a privilege.

On Thursday nights I get kicked out of the house. My wife leads a women's bible study group, and for some reason, I'm not welcome. So most Thursday nights you can find Keith and me sitting near the beach, watching the tide roll away and the sun sink down (cue the Otis Redding song). We talk about recovery, relationships, raising kids, walking free, and people we know who need hope. We talk about God's incredible power and his furious love. We talk about how grateful we are that when both of us felt hopeless, like we were absolutely drowning in sin and dysfunction, Jesus reached down and pulled us up to the surface, and allowed us to breathe deeply.

That's what this book is about. Breathing deeply. Walking free. Surrendering fully and living with hope, passion, purpose, joy, and a peace you can't really adequately explain to people. No one is beyond God's reach. No one.

I hope that you find this story inspiring, and the principles helpful. I pray that your journey will be the same as Keith's. Oh, maybe not a journey from hard core to soft serve, because that's pretty unique. But I hope it's one of surrendering to the love and power of Jesus, so that you can break through the surface … and just breathe.

FROM HARD CORE
TO SOFT SERVE

"PORN STARS WANTED!" There they were, words graffitied in scarlet letters with red spray paint covering the yogurt shop windows. I walked around the corner to see the banners I had proudly displayed on my new store for the whole community to see: "Coming Soon ... Fresh, All Natural ... Surf 'n Yogurt." But the name of the shop was crossed out and covered in red: "PORN PRODUCERS."

I didn't know who wrote it. I didn't know why. It didn't matter. This yogurt shop was supposed to be our starting over. Redeeming this corner of the eclectic neighborhood that was avoided by parents because of the liquor stores and sketchy hotels was going to be our ticket out.

My wife, Samantha, and I had bought a weekend home in Ventura, California, a few years before, looking for a place to get away from the busyness and rush of our lives in Santa Clarita. We enjoyed the little beach town so much that our weekends kept getting longer and longer, blending into weeks. We fell in love with this seaside, surf community. It was such a happy place; everyone exercised—people were always outside running, biking, skateboarding, sailing, and surfing. And everyone was smiling and barefoot; we loved it, and we ended up staying.

We wanted to build something there, so we designed our dream home six houses from the sand, and then my wife had the idea to open a little frozen yogurt shop. We really didn't know much about yogurt, except that we liked to eat it. We knew a lot about running a business, of course, and we decided to give it a shot. We found this little shell of a building that was 390 square feet and located on a busy corner, and it was perfect.

We decorated, printed up beautiful banners to hang outside, and handed out five hundred bright red T-shirts to the local elementary school kids (the most persuading, free advertising you can find), and we were thrilled. Here we were, living in our dream home, and running a new, little family business; life was good.

Until one night I got a call from my friend John. I heard his voice on the other end of the phone, "Keith, you better get over here and look at this. Somebody did something to your shop."

Porn Stars Wanted. Porn Producers. Shame. Embarrassment. Guilt. That's all I could feel; I was overwhelmed, overcome, and buried. I felt sick. How could I be so naive; why did I think we could just start over? I began frantically washing and scraping the windows, and as I washed, it seemed an ironically cruel display of what I had tried to do when I moved here: make all my dirty secrets disappear.

But they hadn't. They had followed me to this place. I had tried so hard to run, so hard to start over, but it's like that old saying, "Wherever you go, there you are," and I had followed me here.

What these people who wrote those words all over my shop didn't understand is that I am not a bad man; I am a business-man. I like to build things, start things, and dream things. And

I had done all three. It's just that my area of business was a little "controversial." I remember all the ways we used to sugar coat it when people would ask what we did. "We're in the film industry," we used to say. "We buy a product and sell it for more than we bought it for," or, "We make instructional videos to help people's marriages." But the truth is: I was a successful businessman in the adult entertainment industry; I created and sold porn. "Adult Entertainment Industry" always seemed to soften it up, but people knew. They always knew what that meant. And so did I.

I knew it meant people would judge me, isolate me—that I would have to hide. I knew it meant that even if people didn't know, I thought they did. It meant my kids wouldn't have play dates and the cop on our street was always watching me and people would feel good about themselves when they spray-painted all over the windows of our new shop.

But, it also meant money, and lots of it. It meant power, wealth, freedom, pride, cars, vacations, houses, and vacation houses. Running this business was all I knew, and I was good at it. We were good at it. My wife was a genius when it came to running the business, and I could sell anything, to anyone. Starting from nothing, with nothing, we built an empire. We owned two companies, the second largest distribution warehouse in the United States and a production company called Devil's Film. Our film company was in the top ten of manufacturers of adult movies and put out two films a week. We were making around three million dollars a year, and I held the respect of my peers and colleagues. I had arrived. We had all we ever wanted, except the only problem was, once we got it, we realized it wasn't what we wanted. And we were tired and empty.

Tired of lying. Tired of hiding. Tired of the games. We wanted our newly adopted son to have a different life than we had given our daughters, and we really thought we could find that in Ventura, if only we could keep our little secret a secret.

But we couldn't. I knew that now. And after washing and scraping away those words all over our shop, I went home to my wife, numb with fear and shame, and told her what happened. I wanted to leave that night, sell everything and get out of this place; it had betrayed me—this once wonderland now felt like hell, and I wanted to run … again. I had started over so many times when things got hard. What made this time any different? But my wife is strong, and in a moment of clarity, she looked up at me, and with determination said, "Go get your bike. We are going for a ride down this street, and we will hold our heads high. We are who we are, and we aren't going anywhere." So we did, and as we rode, I felt like everyone who looked at me was judging me—that they knew all my secrets and that they could see right through me. And it felt like daggers to my heart and soul. But Samantha insisted that we stay.

When I think back to that moment and that we might have left, it overwhelms. Little did I know that little yogurt shop was going to be God's salvation for my family. It was the tool for his perfect plan to change my life.

I don't really like to talk about my life or my past or let people know anything about me, but I heard this guy one time talking about a story from the Bible—this story where some friends of a crippled man carried him to Jesus on a mat. Jesus told the man to get up, take up his mat, and walk. What I will never forget about this story is that Jesus didn't tell him to get up and walk and leave his mat; he told him to get up and carry the mat because he wanted him to remember—remember where he came from and what Jesus had done. Carrying his mat, even when he didn't need it anymore, made people ask him about it, and he would tell them his story about how he couldn't walk and then Jesus healed him.

I was crippled. I was broken, wounded, helpless, and going nowhere, but now I can walk. I was lost, filthy, and broken, but there was a God who loved me anyway. I was lost in the darkness of the porn industry. I was isolated, angry, and addicted, until somebody showed me the light. And all of it—the new house, the draw to the beach, the washing of the letters, and the bike ride—all of it was part of a bigger story of a God who was pursuing me. This is my story. This is my mat.

Part One

The Journey

chapter one

RUBBERLAND

never knew what it felt like to be home. Growing up, I wanted to be normal like the other kids in my school, but my chances were pretty slim from the beginning. Born in Memphis, Tennessee, to two teenagers, I moved in with my grandparents on my dad's side when I was three because my mom's latest husband made me sit in the bathtub while he took my sister in the bedroom and sexually abused her.

My grandmother's house was the first place I met God. The God I met there was distant and strict; my grandmother was Irish Catholic and was firm about us keeping the Ten Commandments. She had rosary beads that dangled above her bed, and she and my grandfather never said the word *love*, which only made my craving for it grow. When I asked her one day if she loved me, she replied, "You show love, you don't say it!" But I had never had anyone say those words to me, and I longed to hear them.

Our house on Bonnie Drive was small, and we were poor; I never had my own room but slept in the den on a foldout cot that was next to the two recliners facing a black and white TV where before bed we all watched *Jeopardy* or shows about normal families. My sister shared a room with my grandmother that had two twin beds separated by a nightstand with a loud Timex wind up clock that we heard ticking at night throughout the house.

I had a heightened curiosity about sex, maybe from the years of living with my mom and abusive stepdad, or maybe just from a deep desire to be wanted. I can still remember looking forward to when I was left in the house alone and sneaked peeks at women in their underwear in the Sears catalogue that my grandmother left on the table. Sometimes my sister did things to me she learned from her abuse, and I saw her get money from the boys at school if she lifted up her top.

When I look back on it now, I feel grateful that my grandparents took me in. I was grateful for the three meals a day, for a place to sleep, and for a routine. We went to the mall with their retired friends, and my sister and I watched cartoons in color on the TV at Sears. We ate our dinner, watched the news at five o'clock, and I went to bed every night at the same time. As we got older, my sister and I rode our bicycles up and down the street, back and forth. Mine was an old bike that my grandfather had found on the railroad tracks; he fixed it up for me, and it had a long banana seat with "sissy bars." He put an ace of spades in the spokes, held on by a clothespin, so when I rode it sounded like a motor.

I remember being driven by my grandparents to school, and I was so embarrassed—not because they were older but because I wished I had a family with a mom and a dad like so many of the other kids. I felt so odd and so different, like an outcast. I wanted to know what it was like to have friends over to my house after school, but I never had one friend over. I never went to anyone else's house either. I created an imaginary world in the backyard where my sister and I played; we called it "Rubberland," and you had to bounce everywhere you went. She was the only friend I had in the world; I felt so alone.

My dad was the town bookie and a firefighter. He drove a long, red Lincoln and wore Elvis sunglasses. He dressed sharp, with a pinky ring and lots of jewelry, and smoked big cigars. I wanted to be just like him. On weekends when I visited him, I marveled at his ultimate bachelor pad. He had a dining room set made out of old wine barrels, a fridge stocked with beer, a pet tarantula, bath towels with letters of our last name monogrammed on them, and porn laid out on the coffee table. He had a round bed with a red velvet comforter and red velvet headboard, and everyone called him, "Handsome Jimmy." He watched sports on the TV all day on Saturday and Sunday, and he cheered for the teams that increased his winnings.

He liked sports, but I was never very good at them. I played baseball once and got the nickname "Smiley." I stood in right field and was so happy I was on a team, I just smiled. I couldn't catch the ball or hit it, and I mainly stayed on the bench. I remember my dad's disappointment once when he threw a ball with me, and I was ball shy. I wanted so badly to prove to him that I could be something and that I could be as successful and as well-liked as he was, but I was a dorky kid with a funny walk and a head too big for my body.

My dad came in and out of the picture. He visited us now and then, but he never stayed for long. On career day at school, when the moms and dads came in and talked about their jobs, I knew my dad's presentation would be the best, if only he showed up. But he never did. One day he promised he would take me fishing and that night I had a dream of turning over leaves trying to find night crawlers, but we never went.

Once he brought us home to live with him and his third wife.

She was not good to us, and we went back to his parents' place. It seemed like he really wanted us there, but his wife didn't; it confused me that he would choose this new wife over us, but I tried not to think about it.

We had lived with my grandparents for ten years when my sister and I starting wondering what it would be like to live with our mom. She had gotten married again, and we began to daydream about the normal family we would have if we lived there. My sister even packed a suitcase and hid it under her bed, hoping that could maybe speed up the process.

When my grandmother found the suitcase under the bed, she was devastated. Hurt, resentful, and angry, she called us in and asked us why we were leaving. My sister told her that we were going to run away and live with our mom, and I'll never forget my grandmother's response. With tears in her eyes, she looked down at us and said, "You don't have to run away. I'll take you first thing tomorrow."

I cried and told her that I didn't want to go; I begged to stay, but what was done was done. I can still hear her crying in the kitchen for what felt like all night, and I barely slept for a moment, hoping she would change her mind. But she didn't, and the next day she took us to our mom's. I realize now, looking back, that that night on my little living room cot was the last night of stability and security that I would have for a long time.

chapter two

"BORN AGAIN"

We left the next morning and went to my mom's, but I think a little piece of me got left behind at Bonnie Drive. When we arrived, I remember feeling all kinds of emotions: sadness, fear, excitement, and hope—all at the same time. Would this, could this possibly be my chance to be normal? To have a family with a mom and a dad who cared about me, took care of me, and loved me—could this be a chance at the life I had always hoped for?

My mom was happy to get us back. She had married a man who was a "born again" Pentecostal Christian. This was an unusual direction for her; I see now that she was just grasping at life, at a home, and at stability—someone or something to make her feel love and a connection. Three of her other children had moved back home, and now there were five of us in the house. This was my mom's fifth husband in twelve years, and he was unlike any of her others; I always wondered if maybe that's why she was drawn to him, hoping he would give her the life she always wanted because he was so religious. But I learned quickly that religion makes you a good person the same way reading about money makes you rich—it doesn't.

Now, in this home, I was exposed to more religion than ever before, but I was never closer to hell.

This God my stepfather knew was demanding and legalistic—like an angry cop waiting around the corner to catch me in the act for the sheer pleasure of it—waiting for me to fail. This God expected us to be at church three nights a week, and my parents fasted every Monday, and there were locks on our cupboard, so that meant we were usually on our own if we wanted to eat. Women couldn't wear pants, only dresses and no makeup, and we weren't allowed to swim with other kids because it would cause us to lust. The prayers people prayed were frightening and forced and in another language I'd never heard; they called it "tongues." There was no TV, no secular music, no Halloween, and no jewelry.

I had been trying for so long to figure out how to let love in, and now everything in our lives revolved around keeping everything I loved out. Every part of our life was filtered through a God who wanted nothing good for me.

It was confusing because I believe my stepfather truly loved and wanted to serve this God, but what I saw didn't match up because he was so fanatically spiritual that it just seemed weird and foreign to me. And I didn't like him. I used to hear them sing that old song "Give Me That Old Time Religion," and all I could think was, *Please don't.*

There were so many of us kids in that little house, and my half-brother Dathan and me were definitely screw-ups from the start. I remember wiping dog poop on the neighbor's car and that sometimes Dathan went into the closet and threw the cat against the wall, overarm and as hard as he could, and that the five of us were terrible to each other. We had little supervision, and we were abusive, mean, hateful and confused, which has left me with many regrets from those years.

Trying to get us under control, my stepfather would take a fiberglass rod from a bicycle, the one that holds the flag, and yelling Scriptures from the Bible at us, he whipped us until we were covered with welts. I suppose he was trying to fix our broken lives, to discipline us to make us better the only way he knew how, but it only made me hate him and want to rebel worse.

Once, he found a Johnny Mathis album in my closet with the single, "Too Much, Too Little, Too Late." It belonged to my mom, but she kept it hidden in my room to keep it from him. When he found it, he beat me, and I let him because I wanted to protect my mom. I was so angry and told him I wanted to go live with my dad. He shoved the phone at me and shouted, "Go ahead, call him; he don't want you!" I called him to prove my stepfather wrong, but he was right. My dad hemmed and hawed on the other end of the line with some excuse why it wasn't a good time for me to come home. I thought how ironic the words of that song were because that is what I felt like I was: too much, too little, too late.

This left me feeling even more alone. I was afraid and resentful. Now in junior high, I fell into deep isolation and depression. I had no idea who I was or where I was going. Insecurity hovered over me at school, and I felt like I didn't matter, like a ghost in the halls—unseen, unnoticed, and inconsequential. I was failing my classes. I was socially awkward and unaccepted. I felt like a loser, and I was lost.

I had to get out, and for once in my life my failure would be my savior.

My stepfather told us kids it was five licks for every F on our report cards. I knew it was going to be bad. Good. Bring it on. My straight Fs and Us were going to be my official "F U" to my step-father. I flunked every class. He beat me so severely I could hardly walk and couldn't sit down the next day. At school, I was sent to the nurse's office, and after one look at my bruises, she immediately called the Department of Child Services. They humiliated me, taking pictures of my naked butt, legs, and lower back, like a wounded animal on a table. They pitied me, but it was a small price to pay for my escape.

That day I was taken from that house and placed in temporary foster care. After the last two years of hell I'd been living, I didn't know where I was going, didn't know what was next, didn't know what I was going to do, but there was one thing I did know: I was walking away from this task-master god and out of the shackles of this house. And I would never let anyone put them on me again.

I had only been in foster care for a short time when my mom's mom, who I affectionately called Grandmugie, and her husband took me in. My grandfather never really said much; he was retired from the Navy and worked a blue collar job in a factory. Grandmugie sold vacuum cleaners, and they attended church.

There was something different about her. She loved me, and she told me she loved me. It was the first time I had ever heard anyone say those three words to me, and I didn't know how to respond. Sometimes I could just hear her say it from the other room at different times throughout the day. She just said, loud enough for me to hear, "I love you, Keith!" I felt like ice was melting inside me. I didn't know what to do or how to answer back; I didn't understand how she could love me when I didn't even love myself!

I had never seen anything like that, felt anything like that before. It took me months before I could respond, not because

I didn't love her but because I didn't know how to love anybody. One day, I finally muscled through the words and said back, "I … love … you … too."

It felt so good to love somebody. So good to be loved by somebody.

Things were starting to look a little brighter for me. Grandmugie sent me to a school called Bethel Baptist, and I started feeling happy and a little more confident and normal. I even decided to sign up for a preaching contest. I practiced my sermon over and over. It was called "Whom God Uses," and Grandmugie sewed me a brand new white suit to wear for the competition. I remember getting on the school bus to go to the Southern Baptist state competition; I had never gotten to do anything like this before, and I was so proud.

And it wasn't like I suddenly started believing in this God I didn't understand, but I started to feel like a part of something and like I might be good at something, which I had never thought would happen. And there I stood to give my sermon. Here I was, this messed up kid, displaced, without a family, neglected, abused, and lost, and I won! I couldn't believe it! It made Grandmugie so proud, and deep down, I was proud of myself too. Pride and love were new feelings for me, and they felt good.

Soon after, there was a candy drive at my school, the kind where you sell candy door-to-door, and I made up my mind that I was going to sell the most candy in the whole school. I went everywhere, knocked on every door I could find, and the night before the contest ended, the sales numbers were tied between me and another girl at school. I remember calling her up to see if she wanted to combine our efforts and split the winnings, and she turned me down. She shouldn't have. Maybe there was something I was good at after all.

Yet, I still wanted, more than anything, to have friends, to be liked, to fit in, and I still just didn't. One day, we had a new student at school named Donny. Donny was my definition of hip, slick, and cool, and for some reason, he wanted to be my friend. We walked home from school together and hung out in the mall and talked to girls. I had no idea how to do that, but after hanging out with Donny and his moves, even girls started to notice me.

One day after school I had my first fight. I didn't know what I was doing, so as we approached the crowd standing around to watch the fight, Donny coached me on what to do. "Hit him in the nose as soon as you walk up," he said, "then finish him." That's exactly what I did. It felt really good to win, and suddenly it seemed like I fit in.

Donny introduced me to girls, and he also introduced me to drugs. He showed me how to smoke weed, and we partied. I thought Donny's parents were awesome; they didn't care if he smoked, and if he stole from them they either never noticed or never said anything.

One night, when I was seventeen, we went to the gravel pits and met some girls. Donny had sex with a girl in the back of a car, and when he was done, he asked her if she'd have sex with me too so I could lose my virginity. I don't remember her name, but Donny called her "sloppy seconds." When we got home, he told his parents, and the three of them laughed at me because it had taken me so long to lose my virginity. When I was at Donny's place, I could do anything and everything I wanted, so I stopped coming home to Grandmugie.

But she didn't stand for it. She was strong and cared about me; she told me I needed to stop doing drugs and hanging out with Donny or she'd kick me out. And as much as I loved her and loved her love for me, it just wasn't enough to keep me from this new life I'd found. I left, and Donny's parents took me in and became my foster parents.

After the move, I enrolled in a public school, but every day we skipped school and smoked weed and drank beer all afternoon. The older kids in the school taught us how to roll joints. I rolled on my way to school to sell when I got there, and that became my only reason for showing up.

My life was going downhill fast. The drinking had become more frequent and the drugs more extreme—I was doing acid and speed—anything I could get my hands on. My parents were out of the picture; I had only seen my dad for a minute one day when he hunted me down after I went to his house and stole a bunch of jewelry for us to pawn so my friends and I could party.

While high and drunk one afternoon, we decided to go visit Donny's grandfather in the hospital. Afterward, I went down the hall and waited for the elevator. I lit up a cigarette, and when the elevator opened, my mom's sister was standing right in front of me. She looked at me, surprised, and asked if I was there to see my mom.

I stood there, a punk of a kid, showing them I could smoke in front of them because I could do whatever I wanted. But the only thing that came out of my mouth was, "Why?"

I had only seen my mom once after I had been taken away, after she had gotten a divorce and was living in government housing. I randomly had decided to stop by, and I sat with her and drank beers and talked. That was the last time I saw her.

"She had a stroke from a brain aneurism," my aunt said. "One side exploded, and the left side of her body was paralyzed. Then the other side exploded, and she went into a coma."

I walked over to the front desk to try and find her room. When I got there, she lay motionless in the bed, her hair ratty with glue from the wires attached to track her brain waves. The left side of her face was bloody from where she had scratched it but couldn't feel it. She was lifeless, helpless, motionless, and in that moment, I felt exactly the same way. The moment I saw her, all my anger melted out of me and gathered at my feet, like a pool on the hospital floor. All I felt was pain.

"Mama, I love you." Those were my broken words, the only words I could manage to utter as I held her hand, holding back uncontrollable sorrow. I began to yell, "Mama, can you hear me? I love you!" And right when I said those words, the heart monitor went flat, she took her last breath, and she died, right there, with her hand wrapped in mine.

I sat outside the curtain around her bed as the nurses cleaned her up and took away all the wires and monitors. All I could think of was to ask for the wristband that had her name on it. They handed it to me, and it felt like the weight of a thousand bricks, and as I walked out of that hospital, I felt a heaviness deep within my soul, creating a bitterness that propelled me deeper into hiding. I had to get away from that pain, and I was ready to do whatever it took.

I've heard it said that what comes to our minds when we think about God is the most important thing about us. I guess it's because when we see God as distant and strict and demanding and waiting for us to fail, we become distant, scared, and weak failures. I didn't like this God I met in my childhood, didn't like this God that put me in the room right when my mom took her last breath, but it was OK because I was pretty sure he didn't like me much either.

chapter three

STARVING FOR LOVE

I don't remember much about my mom's funeral. I drove in with my cousin, and we were smoking weed and drinking. I do remember looking into her face as she lay in the casket. She looked so empty and lifeless, and it made me wonder about death, about the point of her life, and about the point of mine. I remember my stepdad coming up to me and saying, "If she had stayed with me and not wandered away from the Lord, this wouldn't have happened to her." And it made me so angry—at him, at God, at me, and at her.

Is that really why she died? How could God expect that of her—to stay with such an abusive man and not have failures or make mistakes? Who was this God who just took a life that didn't measure up to his never-ending ruler? I felt like he stood as a judge, black robe and gavel and all, and he just sat somewhere up in the sky waiting for me to fail. But it didn't make me fear him; it made me hate him.

I was still starving for love and finding it however I could, and when I told people about my mom's death, they gave me such compassion, seemed to genuinely care about me, and gave me sympathy. And I realized quickly that playing this victim of my mother's death actually became a tool to get whatever I wanted. You didn't have to know me for more than five minutes before I poured out my soul and the pain of my mother's death, especially if you were a pretty girl.

I was seventeen years old and still floating around without a purpose, trying to find my way when my dad's roommate moved out and my dad offered me a place to stay. Because he was a firefighter and worked twenty-four hours at a time, I often brought girls to the house to party, have sex, and get wasted. Since Dad was a bookie, he always had lots of cash lying around the house. I often peeled back a couple of twenties from the wad he kept on his dresser; he never noticed.

My dad married a beautiful blonde who was only a couple years older than me, and they invited me to move in with them. They slept in my dad's old roommate's room and gave me the red velvet bed. I don't know if she felt like I was her little brother or her stepson, but she and my dad started trying to help me restart my life. She drove me to night school across town to help me get my GED, and my dad got me a full-time job at a factory. I started paying rent, which they were going to give back to me so I could even get my own car. It started looking like something good was happening in my life again—that I might even have a future.

It only took me a couple of months though, before I started to get off track. At night school, I started smoking weed with cute girls while skipping class to go drinking. I always made sure I was back in time for my ride home.

One night I snuck out of my window and went to a store and stole a pack of cigarettes and got caught. They called my dad and told him I was in jail, and he vouched for me, saying it was impossible because I was asleep in the other room. It only took him opening the door to see that I had figured out how to open the window that had been screwed shut, so he came and picked me up.

I started meeting guys at work who sold me speed, and one day my dad found the drugs in the pocket of my coat that was hanging in the closet. He was so angry he began yelling and threatening me, chasing me through the house until I locked him out of my room. I called the Department of Child and Family Services on him, and they showed up the next day, which shocked and hurt him.

There I sat as they walked through the house, investigating and asking my dad all kinds of questions. Finally, he just looked at them and said, "Pack his stuff and take him with you! If you can do better, have at it!" I could tell by the look on their faces that this was an unusual response from a parent, but they could tell that I wasn't in danger and was just a kid trying to get revenge on his dad.

I stayed until three days before my eighteenth birthday when I came home and found all my stuff packed and sitting on the porch. I had bought a car from my stepmother, which allowed me even more time for self-destructive trouble. They had had enough. I threw my stuff in the trunk, left, and never looked back.

I had a car, a job, and freedom. I started drinking and doing more drugs. I was staying out all night with my friends and was sleeping in my car. I took speed pills to get through my eight-hour shifts at the factory, and they helped me stay awake. But my work, understandably and noticeably, started to slip. My general manager started worrying about me, and when I told him I was homeless, he offered to let me crash at his place for a while.

Homelessness didn't threaten me; I had felt homeless most of my life, even when I was living in a house. Nevertheless, I took him up on his offer, and I liked living at his place; he gave me my own room, and we smoked pot and drank beer together. We sang and played music for hours every night. He promoted me at work, and I loved my independence.

Being my boss, he made more money than I did, but he didn't seem to mind sharing his lifestyle with me. Eventually, I remember feeling like I needed my space. I started hooking up with girls for the night, coming home less and less.

My erratic schedule and lack of time with him seemed to irritate him, but when he'd bring it up, I ignored him; I knew he was jealous of the amount of girls I was sleeping with, and I brushed him off. One night after a heated argument about where I had been so late, he grabbed me and began to touch me, molesting and assaulting me. In that moment, I realized he hadn't been jealous of me but jealous of them. He had warped and twisted our relationship, and it freaked me out. I left and never returned.

As much as this incident scared me, shamed me, and completely humiliated me, it mostly reminded me that I was on my own, that I could trust no one, and that I had no one. No one cared about me, and no one loved me. I had no mother, no father, no friends, and no family. It was in this utter loneliness that I got a call from my half-brother Dathan.

I hadn't seen him since my mom's funeral. He was homeless too, and I figured as long as we were both alone, we might as well be alone together.

It was nice to be with some sort of family. After I left my boss's house, I had tried to find my sister, but she was a stripper and doing meth and couldn't take me in. Dathan and I just sort of stuck together. We drove around and lived in his stolen car, wandering from place to place trying to figure out how to get money. We stole a little here and there; I remember staying at someone's house and stealing all their gold coins. We even took the glass bottles that people were saving on their porches to return for money. We used this small amount of cash for gas money, beer, and drugs—but we mostly just drove around and came up with scams to get what we needed.

We took old dish soap bottles and filled them with hot salt water and squirted them into the coin slots in soda machines. For some reason, it made all the cans fall out of the machine, and the change dispenser empty out. Then, we resold the soda to the corner liquor store.

All we had was time, and it was starting to get old. Our care-free life was getting tiresome; we were spinning in circles and getting nowhere.

One morning I was waiting for my brother to come pick me up, and he was taking an unusually long time. When he finally arrived, he walked up to me on foot. "Where you been?" I asked. "I wrecked my car," he said, standing there, pathetic looking with all of his belongings stuffed in a single duffle bag. Now we had no way to get anywhere, no way to scam money for our addictions, nowhere to sleep; we were busted. That's when I remembered the girl from California.

Her name was Angie. After we had partied together one night, she gave me her number and said if I was ever in California I should look her up. I wasn't in California yet, but I decided to look her up anyway; we had to get out of Memphis. We managed to scam enough money for two one-way bus tickets—from Memphis to Los Angeles—with three dollars left over for some cigarettes and whisky for the ride.

The possibilities were endless. I really thought we could go there and escape our past. I knew this was our chance to start over. We put almost two thousand miles and five states in-between us and all that had happened, or didn't happen, in our life. And it felt great.

The ride was long. It felt like we stopped in every town, like we were never going to get there. I was so hungry and so tired, rotating between drinking and sleeping it off. People kept talking to us, some of them even about God, which just made me angry. I thought they were crazy and only indulged their conversation because I was hoping they would give us something to eat.

When we arrived in LA, we had never seen anything like it! Our bus dropped us off on 7th Street, and we had no money. All I had left was a quarter-karat pinky ring that my dad had given to me. I sold it to someone in the bus station, and this allowed us a grand arrival in LA.

I found a payphone and called Angie. I could sense her surprise on the other end of the phone. I knew she lived in Palmdale, but I had no idea where that was or how long it would take for her to get to us. She told me it would take a couple hours to get there, so Dathan and I went to find some food.

We found a bar on the corner that looked like it had food, but the biggest draw was the beautiful California blondes we saw sitting inside. It only took my brother a few drinks to get up the courage to go talk to one of them, and it only took moments for the two of them to hit it off. I felt like we had just arrived in the Promised Land.

The bartender handed me another drink, and I glanced up at him and remarked at what a great city LA was. "Man, I can't believe this; we've been here less than an hour and my brother has already hooked up with a beautiful woman!"

The bartender paused and looked back at me with a smirk and a raised eyebrow, "You serious?" he said. I looked at him, confused. "That beautiful woman ain't no woman," he said. It took me a moment to realize what he meant, but as soon as I did, I spun around and stared at the Adam's apple on the beautiful woman my brother was kissing.

I ran over to the table and ripped Dathan's arm away from their embrace, "Let's go!" I whispered. "What are you doin'?" he said, shocked and angry at the interruption. I just looked back and said, "She's a dude!"

He got up from the table so fast, and we both bolted out of the bar and ran around the corner. I was laughing hysterically at him. He was stunned, like he had just been abruptly awakened from a deep sleep. But I just kept laughing.

As we stood in the alley, me doubled over with laughter, him wiping his mouth with his sleeve, a man walked up to us. "Hash?" he asked, holding out a wad of marijuana wrapped in aluminum foil.

We made the exchange with the money we had left, saving only enough for a bottle of beer to wash it down, and off he went into the sea of people on the crowded LA sidewalk. And there we were, unwrapping and unwrapping and unwrapping, discarding one small sheet of foil after another until we reached the last, finding nothing inside.

Angry and empty handed, we began to run aimlessly through the crowd, looking for our supplier, but he was long gone and probably somewhere counting his money and laughing at the guys so obviously from out of town.

We were having a rough start.

Once we finally got picked up, I remember waking up to beauty like I'd never seen: mountains with snowy caps landscaped the desert terrain that was filled with Joshua trees and tumble-weeds. I fell so in love with this place, I even wrote a poem:

> Well I'm just a guy from Tennessee
> Can hardly write and can barely read
> Came to California you see
> To see all I'd been watchin' on TV
> There's mountains and desert land
> A whole lot of tumbleweeds
> A whole lot of sand.

chapter four

I WISH
YOU WERE HERE

People were different in California. Everyone wore button-fly jeans, listened to Madonna, and smoked clove cigarettes. They talked different too, taking pride that they were from the Valley. I loved it.

I started meeting people like this and making as many friends as I could find. Connections became my life. I carried two little black books in my back pockets everywhere I went to keep track of all the numbers. I had sections for girls, jobs, and weed, which pretty much defined what mattered most to me.

I had never known people like this before, and I never had so many friends and so many possibilities. My life was blooming. The little town I was in was booming. Construction was everywhere, and I found out we could get jobs as laborers on a construction site starting at ten dollars per hour.

The next morning, I woke Dathan and made him get dressed. "I have an idea," I said, and we walked down to the local store and bought a pair of work boots, a tool bag, a tape measure, and a hammer. We went out back and dropped our tool bags in the dirt, roughing them up, convinced the new scuffs made us look like we had been carpenters all our lives. I figured if we wanted to get jobs, we couldn't look like rookies.

We slung them over our shoulders and began to walk down the road, hitchhiking, hoping someone would hire us. "Think this will work?" Dathan asked me as we walked. I felt a heavy weight at his question, like a cross between resentment and fear at his dependence on me and at his need for me to provide. I wanted to run.

I lit up a cigarette and said, "We'll see," just as a guy pulled up in a truck and offered us a ride to a work site. It worked, and we kept it up every day. The work was hard and exhausting, but it paid cash and that was all that mattered to us.

We were soon evicted from Angie's house. After her mom started to leave for work one morning and found that her car was gone, she came inside in a panic, frantic that her car had been stolen, until that afternoon when my brother nonchalantly pulled up in the driveway like he had just been out running some errands. We were done and homeless again.

I met a new girl and moved in with her, which brought some distance between Dathan and me. He ended up getting a bus ticket and moved back to Tennessee, and I decided to move up into the mountains. There was a national park back in the mountains nestled between Palmdale and Little Rock, and about a mile past the dam was a little store that sold beer, cigarettes, and food. It had a seated bar for drinking and eating, and it had two cabins behind it. I lived in the cabin on the left and ran the store.

It was a beautiful place and in the summer, people from the city came up on the weekends (by the thousands) to drink, camp, go four-wheeling, and party. I knew everyone, it seemed, and, of course, I was holding—weed, acid, and cocaine. I had it all, and all we did was drugs, sex, and nothing. Girls begged to stay at my place, just so they could wake up and see the sunrise the next morning, and I graciously obliged. It was a circus, and I was the Master of Ceremonies, and I loved it.

Albert Einstein once said that the definition of insanity is doing the same thing over and over again and expecting different results. I'm no Einstein, but I was beginning to see that played out in my life. Over and over again, I created this pattern of starting over: having fun, making connections, having too much fun, winning people over, doing drugs, selling drugs, and having everyone love me. Then it got less fun, and everyone would leave me. And I moved on.

The morning the park rangers came to my house, I was sitting on the floor, stoned. It was a one-room cabin with a makeshift mattress in the corner where I slept with a wool blanket and a pillow. Across the hardwood floors sat a potbelly stove, a wooden chair, a green card table, and a small plastic bucket with water from the store that I brought to wash my hands and hair. There was light blue material hanging over the window, and it was usually quiet. But not that morning.

BAM, BAM, BAM! There was a pounding on my door that echoed off the log walls of my cabin. "Open the door, sir." How long had they been knocking? I dreaded the light coming in when I opened the door, so I didn't.

BAM, BAM, BAM!

"What do you want?" I yelled back. They answered with more banging, so I opened the door. I was right about the light. They informed me that I had to leave or they would force me to. They knew I was selling coke. I knew that they knew, and I left.

Making my way back down to Palmdale, I had nothing. I was

busted: homeless again, no gas for my car, and nowhere to go anyway. I decided to just park my car and camp in a park—backpack for a pillow and the sky for a blanket. It wasn't bad. I found a place that gave out free food, and I had a box that I hid in the bushes to sleep in for shelter at night. I gathered sticks during the day and burned them at night.

I spent my days in the park partying with the teenagers until my luck and friendships once again ran out. I heard that there was a General Relief office for the homeless and hungry in Lancaster; I went to the office to apply. I had to get there early to take a number. The room was full, and the line was long. Applying took as long as a day's work, so I made use of it, talking to girls, most of them moms with kids, but they had homes and cars and food stamps. I tried to charm them enough to enjoy at least a night off my back in the park.

I met a girl and someone told us of a hotel in town called the Yogi that took vouchers. We went there together and found a two-story hotel, long and narrow, nestled behind the post office, off Lancaster Boulevard. We walked through the door and found the front desk, with a little room off to the side that served as the living quarters for the person in charge. The manager gave us a key, and said our room was on the second floor. As he pushed a button under the counter, an annoying, loud buzz filled my ears.

I thought about the irony of that buzzer. Who were they trying to keep out? Everyone who anyone was afraid of was inside these walls—the balding woman with the hairless cat that stared at you when you walked by, a woman screaming from a beating, pimps, addicts, and people mentally, emotionally, and physically disturbed. It was terrible.

As I walked down the hallway to my room, I noticed the co-ed, prison-like showers and wondered if anyone ever felt safe in this place. I quickly shoved my key in the knob of my room. It smelled like mildew and body odor, and I started to long for the fresh air of the park. In my room there was a bed in the corner with a white sheet and a thin, washed-too-many-times blanket. I shared a bathroom with my new neighbor, and behind the door there was a closet without a door. Everything was white—white paint covered in white paint—and I saw a little sink with a small mirror above it. I glanced at myself and quickly looked away, tossed my bag on the floor and lay down on the bed, looking up and watching the roaches race across the ceiling.

I guess this is home, I thought. *It'll work.*

Of course, I immediately started making connections within this new world of welfare at the Yogi Hilton, especially with two guys named Richard and Jake, and we soon became known as the Three Musketeers of the Yogi with the nicknames Ricky Welfare, Jake the Snake, and Keith the Thief.

We began to make a way of life around these identities. A soup truck came twice a week and gave us free soup, and I could feed the whole hotel with bags of trash from McDonald's. Or we'd swing by the AM/PM and grab a "flat pack" (our self-named hamburgers because we bagged two burgers and flattened them down so we could get two for the price of one). We paid two bucks for a flat pack and a malt liquor beer, the breakfast of champions. Richard, Jake, and I went to the liquor stores with our food stamps and took turns buying twenty-cent candy. They gave us our change in cash, and we saved up enough to buy beer, a reward for all our hard work.

My charm had earned me a great connection at the unemployment office and a lady there called me daily with "spot jobs," and we took them, mostly because they paid cash. And cash meant we could still collect from the welfare office. The jobs never lasted for more than a week, but they were enough for us.

Then I met Johnny Cash. Johnny Cash didn't look anything like the real Johnny Cash, and he was a pimp. He had two girls, and he liked me. He let me come along during his collections. I remember him screaming at one of his girls who had bought a burger from the gas station, "Girl, did I say you could eat a burger?" He grabbed it and threw it on the ground. I thought it was funny, and at the end of the night, he took me to Pizza Hut to split a large pizza and a pitcher of beer. Johnny Cash became my idol.

There was a woman on the second floor with cancer—she had lost her hair and eyebrows and always wore a wrap around her head. One night my friend Jake went into her room while she slept and stole two thousand dollars from her. We were drunk and happy as we divided up the money. We bought speed and checked into another hotel, partying for three or four days straight. We returned, broke and guilty, but denied everyone's accusations.

After that, I moved into Cindy's room, the girl from the welfare office. I used her for her car, double food stamps, and sex, in that order. We cooked in our room and washed our dishes in the hand sink. I treated Cindy badly, taking her car out with my friends all night to go drink at bars and hit on women. I wore a necklace with all the rings I collected from the girls I met, and I sang in front of her, "To all the girls I loved before, I'm openin' my own jewelry store."

One morning, Cindy told me she was pregnant. She said it was mine, but I wasn't sure because I knew she had been with Jake and at least one other guy since we'd been together. But the pregnancy brought with it one reward: more food stamps and government aid. I had gotten a job at a grocery store, but took off my apron and walked out when I found that out. I had a hard time holding down a regular job anyway, especially since most nights I was up all night drinking and doing drugs.

Cindy and I were together for six months into her pregnancy when we lost our room at the Yogi. We moved in with a friend of hers in Palmdale. We lived in a duplex, and her friend had two kids and liked to party. I ended up becoming a babysitter while they went out. It made me angry. One night I called up my friend from down the street, Cookie, and we met up at the Vagabond Motel on Palmdale Boulevard. We drank, went in the hot tub, and did drugs until the sun came up. I told her all about my unhappiness, and she told me I could move in with her and her mom. I did, and I never looked back—never even found out if Cindy had the baby.

Cookie and I lived in a studio apartment in Palmdale. I was "a buck twenty-five" soaking wet, with a mullet. We spent our days slamming drugs and eating food that I gathered out of trash cans. Our apartment was a shooting gallery, junkies coming in to shoot up, hide their syringes, and get high. We were their first stop when they were let out of prison and their last stop before they went back in.

I wanted to go back to Memphis. California was expensive, and all I could think about was Grandmugie and her house and how she was kind and generous and had loved me once. Maybe she still did. I told Cookie about the kind of woman Grandmugie was and how I had family there and that my dad lived on a lake. Like every addict, I knew if we could just start over, we could *start over* and our demons wouldn't follow us there.

I had a truck that I was trying to sell, and Cookie started cleaning house for an old man in our neighborhood. I encouraged her to clean in her underwear to get extra money so we could get a bus ticket back to Memphis.

Once we arrived in Memphis, I reunited with my brother Dathan, and the three of us were inseparable.

We liked being together. It was us against the world. I remember one night hitchhiking from bar to bar. We held out our thumbs and a nice man pulled over and let us in. "Where you headed?" Bob said with a friendly grin as the three of us jumped in his car. After a couple of miles, Dathan told him we were good. "You can pull over here, this is our stop," he said. Cookie and I leaned up to get out, but before we could, Dathan reached over, grabbed the keys from the ignition, and pulled out a knife. "I hate to be bogus, Bob," he said, "but I'm gonna have to take your wallet."

Bob was terrified and shocked. So were we. We had no idea he was going to rob this guy, but Dathan was unpredictable. After grabbing his wallet, we all jumped out of the car, and my brother tossed Bob's keys as far as he could. We left Bob there and walked away, sifted through the wallet, tossed out the credit cards, kept the cash, and headed to the bar.

We lived in an area where crime and poverty were high, and everywhere you went was unsafe. Racial tensions were high in Memphis, and we were always the minority. We did whatever it took to score the drugs we needed. We rode down the street, Dathan driving, Cookie in the middle, and me in the passenger seat. I cracked my window a few inches as we drove real slow. Guys rushed to the car, stuck in their hand with the drugs, and we exchanged it for cash.

On days we didn't have cash, we played the same game, but instead of exchanging the drugs for cash, we hit their hand so the drugs fell to the floorboard. We floored it, driving away laughing about our score. One time, the window wasn't up far enough, and the dealer punched me in the side of my head, just as Dathan got punched on the other side of the car. Both our heads hit Cookie's, and Dathan floored the gas as we tore away with gunshots leaving bullet holes in our car.

But this was how we filled our days, getting high, running, hiding, escaping, and going nowhere. Nothing had changed for us. We were the same people as before, except we were in a new place, and now I was just doing things in closer proximity to Grandmugie. As hard as my heart was, breaking Grandmugie's still hurt me.

Grandmugie wanted Cookie and me to get married. She didn't like us living together, and if we stayed in her house, she made us sleep in separate bedrooms. We decided to honor her wishes. On the day of our wedding, I was out scoring drugs in downtown Memphis in the projects with Dathan, and he went around the back of the store to take a leak. Out of nowhere, he was jumped by three guys, and they started chasing him. The next thing I knew the five of us were boxing in the parking lot. I showed up to Grandmugie's church late and high, with a swollen black eye. I was late for my own wedding.

Cookie and I rented an apartment and tried to make a life for ourselves. My aunt and Grandmugie bought us curtains and silverware and a couch for our tiny living room. But no matter how much we tried to make a go at a new life, the drugs and alcohol always got in the way. Cookie enrolled in night school to get her high school diploma, but I knew it was just so she could get it and have the power she needed to leave me.

While she was in school, I was out running the streets with my brother. We got drunk and robbed cars one by one in the parking lot, stole stuff out of people's front lawns and broke into the laundromat's washers and dryers to get change—anything to get more drugs and alcohol. We visited my sister at work where she was a stripper and tried to get cash. One night, after pleading with us to leave, she ended up doing a hit of acid with us. When my dad came and got her, she was frying and lay on his bed staring at the ceiling all night tripping on LSD. We just sat there and laughed.

Cookie got sick and had to go to the hospital. I just kept partying. Sick with jaundice and scared and alone in the hospital, she called and pleaded with me to come stay with her. "I ain't gonna come up there!" I joked back, "I hear you're as yellow as a canary!" I hung up and took a hit. I didn't care about anybody or anything. I was thoughtless and inconsiderate and mean. I had stopped feeling anything for anybody; it was easier to bury thoughts and emotions than experience them, and partying and escaping was not a part of my life—it *was* my life. It was all that mattered and all that I wanted to do.

One day, our little dream of a life literally went up in smoke when we had a cooking fire in our apartment that destroyed everything. The curtains that had once been so hopeful of a bright future were now black. A metaphor for our life: dark, broken, and unlivable.

Nothing was working. Every day was the same. I had three DUIs, and we decided to move. Dathan had an uncle up in Jackson, Tennessee, who owned a siding company. Dathan called him up to ask if we could come live with him and work for him.

Excited about the cheap labor, his uncle said, "Come on up!" Grandmugie was happy to drive us up to the edge of the city line of Memphis and let us out, all three of us.

The way we lived our lives reminds me of something I read the other day in the Alcoholics Anonymous' *Big Book*:

> The alcoholic is like a tornado roaring his way through
> the lives of others. Hearts are broken. Sweet relationships
> are dead. Affections have been uprooted. Selfish and

inconsiderate habits have kept the home in turmoil. We feel a man is unthinking when he says that sobriety is enough. He is like the farmer who came up out of his cyclone cellar to find his home ruined. To his wife, he remarked, "Don't see anything the matter here, Ma. Ain't it grand the wind stopped blowin'?"*

This was our lives. Sometimes I wonder about Grandmugie's drive back home. She must have been relieved. Must have been sad. Must have been angry. Maybe she still cared. Maybe she still loved me. Maybe she said a prayer, but I fear there was a big part of her that was relieved the storm had moved on.

But, we hadn't been in Jackson long before the hurricane of our haphazard lives hit again; after all, wherever you go, there you are. We didn't have a car, didn't have money, but we were resourceful enough to find drugs. We were in a rough area when Dathan walked across the street, and I saw him talking to a guy. Suddenly, I saw my brother grab this guy by the crotch and say, "You want me to let go? You better give me some drugs."

The man handed him some drugs, and Dathan ran across the street where five guys attacked him. Watching and wondering if I should help, I suddenly saw his hand reach out of the scuffle. "Keith … take em!" he yelled, holding up the drugs. Before I could react, the guys got the drugs and for some reason just let Dathan go.

That was everyday living for us.

Things were not going well with Cookie. She had become distant, and I was mean, abusive, and hateful. She wanted out, and I didn't know how to love her. We were in a drug-induced relationship from the beginning, and nothing had changed. We were both looking for love and hated ourselves.

---

* Bill W. and Bob Smith, *Alcoholics Anonymous* (New York City: Alcoholics Anonymous World Services, Inc., 2006), 82.

Then I found out that Cookie and Dathan were having an affair. On the surface, I felt betrayed and angry, but deep down I knew I had not been good to her. After finding out, Dathan and I got in a vicious fight. In the midst of our yells and curses, he grabbed a knife and stabbed my neck, right through my jugular vein. Gushing blood, I yelled, "I'm gonna kill you!" I finally made it to the hospital, and I couldn't lift my head for three weeks.

When Cookie finally told me she was going to leave, I couldn't take it. I was at the end of hope, and I attempted suicide. Looking back, I know that it wasn't her leaving me that hurt. I didn't blame her; it was that I just didn't want to be alone. I was so alone. No friends. No family. No home. As soon as Cookie got the money, she left and flew back to California.

Dathan and I stayed in Jackson and were working for Dathan's uncle putting vinyl siding on a house and crashing at an extra place he had. One night we borrowed his van and were out drinking and got pulled over. They arrested Dathan and took him to jail, and I hid in the bushes until I thought they were gone. Jumping in the driver's seat, I peeled away, and as soon as I took off, I saw flashing lights in the rearview mirror. Dathan and I slept in the same cell that night.

The next morning, we were in court facing our sentence when the bailiff leaned over and whispered something to the judge. Instantly, the case was dismissed, and we were free to go. Turns out the house that was getting new siding belonged to the bailiff.

This was my fourth DUI in Jackson, following my third, which was technically a "BUI" (boating under the influence). I had tried to throw the beers in the water as the Harbor Patrol pulled up alongside me, but I didn't realize beer cans floated, and they just grabbed the cans out of the water and put them in the hull of their boat.

Too humiliated to return to Dathan's uncle's house, we walked out of jail and hitchhiked right out of town back to Memphis.

When we got there, Dathan and I scrounged up enough money to get a station wagon that became our transportation, home, and business. We started a little business called "Two Brother's Siding" to try and make money but nothing had changed; we just spent whatever we made on drugs.

Somehow, we ended up getting an apartment with my sister, and I slept with some guy's wife. He was always coming over and banging on the door late at night and fighting with me. I got another DUI one night on a motorcycle some girl loaned me, with her on the back. They took me to jail and walked me down to the cellblock. I was a skinny, little, white guy with a pretty, bleached blonde rat tail down the center of my back. And the bailiff yelled out to a cell with about fifty black guys, "Hey, you all got any white boys in there?"

"Yeah, we got some white boys in here! Bring him on in!" There were no white boys in there.

I sat there all day watching as these guys fought each other for fun, cheered on the winners, laughed at the losers, and I was terrified. I tried to keep to myself when the largest of them walked over to me and said, "Come twelve o'clock, you gonna have to be a man, or you gonna have to be a boy ... but you gonna have ta be some'n."

Only moments later I heard the jailer shout, "Repult, roll it up!" I was bailed out by some guy my sister was dating. I knew I had skipped bond on the four DUI's in Jackson, and I expected to be extradited, but somehow I caught a break. I remember trying to act cool. But my swagger turned to a stride that turned to a strut that took me right to the liquor store. I was thirsty and picked up right where I had left off.

As soon as I had a drink, I hooked up with Dathan, and we needed money. We decided to rob someone's house, and I wrapped my arm with a coat and broke the glass out of the door. We stole the TV and a VCR and ran out of the house with our arms full.

We heard, "HOLD IT ... POLICE!" We dropped everything and ran. Hiding all night, we managed to escape, but this time we weren't getting away. The police raided Grandmugie's house and put a warrant out for my arrest. I decided to move down to Mississippi with my dad, which meant leaving Dathan.

I had a deep love for my brother, but I had no idea how to show him. It was a sick and broken love, a codependent and destructive love. He was my younger brother, and I should have taken care of him. But I was lost. He was lost. We were lost, together.

I said goodbye and thought about the Pink Floyd song we'd heard and sung so many times together, radio blaring and off key with the windows rolled down, "Just two lost souls swimming in a fishbowl, year after year, running over the same old ground, what have we found? The same old fears ... wish you were here."

That was us. Spinning, whirling, and out of control. Living to use, so dying. We were miserable together, and I knew the best thing for him would be for me to leave. Soon after, Dathan met a nice girl and decided to get married and start over ... again.

I wasn't in Mississippi long before my dad began pleading with me to turn myself in. Afraid that he might do it for me, and knowing that it would mean over a year in prison, I decided to return to California.

I got a bus ticket and called Cookie, and she was waiting at the bus stop when I arrived. We lived with her mom until we quickly got kicked out. We moved to Lancaster and stayed in the back of a tow truck company because the guy who owned it liked Cookie.

High and drunk one night, I answered the phone. It was Dathan's father.

"Dathan's dead." The words whirled in my foggy head.

It happened the day after his wedding. He walked down that same old street in Memphis, but this time without me. His new wife was at work, and he went out to score a quarter gram of coke. Running away from the dealer, he was shot in the back of the head and died on the curb.

I begged his dad to buy me a ticket so I could come back for his funeral. He said no, and I cried all night long; it broke my heart that I lost him. Still to this day, I think about how he never got that chance, about how short and broken and hopeless his life was, and I can't help thinking, *Wish you were here.*

chapter five

KINKY KEITH

ookie got a job waitressing at a place called Spankies, and I sold drugs. I showed up at her work one night looking to sell and looking to drink. There was a man sitting at the bar wearing a fur coat and a gold rope chain around his neck with a gold medallion in the center. He was on his cell phone, which was connected by a cord to a box the size of a radio hanging from a strap and resting on his hip.

He reached into his pocket and pulled out a wad of hundred-dollar bills. *This guy needs some drugs,* I thought, and sat down next to him.

"Hey, what's happening … you need some drugs?"

"No, I don't need no drugs," he said.

"Well, buy me a drink."

He looked back, annoyed, "Get a job."

"I'm looking for a job," I lied to get him to feel sorry for me and buy me a drink.

"What do you do?"

"I'm a carpenter." I'd done my fair share of carpentry work

by now; during the 80s the housing market was booming, and I could walk off one construction job and on to another, so I figured I could officially call myself a carpenter.

He said, "Be at my store in the morning, and you can build me some shelves."

He bought me a drink, and gave me a card with the address of his store. It was called Sunshine Gifts, an adult bookstore that sold magazines, DVDs, toys, and pipes, and it sounded cool. I thought, *This guy has got it going on!*

The next morning, I showed up with my tool bag, and he put me to work. I built shelves in his store, and he was impressed. "I've got another store in Lancaster and four doors down from that store is an empty warehouse. I want you to build some shelves there too."

The one thousand square foot warehouse was empty when I arrived, and I didn't know what he was planning to do with it. He told me to build more shelves, so I did. I liked working for this guy. His name was Greg, and I loved hanging out with him because he had money and took care of me, often paying me in cash, beer, and weed.

Once the shelves were built, he invited me to come with him to the Valley to pick up the product we were going to put on them. "I'm not gonna pay you, but if you want to ride along, I'll buy you lunch. We'll smoke some weed, and you can just come and hang out with me as a friend," he said.

I had no friends, and nothin' else to do, so I was in. He took me to a strip club on our way down, and when we arrived to pick up the product for the empty shelves, the warehouse was full of porn.

I didn't know where to look. Rows and rows of adult movies of every kind I could ever imagine. I decided to keep my eyes straight on the ground. I repeated over and over in my head, *Don't look, don't look,* but glanced out of the side of my eye, so at least he wouldn't see me look.

We bought our inventory and took it back and loaded up the shelves. Greg looked at me as we unloaded the boxes, "Now that we've got this, I'll need a shipper. Want to be a shipper?"

"What's it pay?" I responded, as if I had better offers waiting. He told me it paid $3.35 per hour. "I've got nothing else to do," I responded. And so I began working for Greg. He sold and I shipped. I packed, manually logged the inventory line by line, weighed and taped the box, added the address and sent the product to stores around the country.

Greg sat on the phone all day with adult bookstores from all around the country. He could sell, and I loved listening to him. He had relationships with people, and he knew them by name. He'd call Rosy from Texas, "Hey, Rosy, it's Dirty Greg …" and he read her every title of everything new, and he sold it all.

Every day around three o'clock, it was beer time; we drank and smoked weed. It was too late to make calls because he called overseas or back East, so we packed orders together for the next day, worked until around five o'clock, and then drank, smoked weed, and ate until ten o'clock.

One night we partied too hard, and Greg didn't show up the next morning. Since it was just me, I decided that maybe I should try and make some sales. I went over to his desk and picked up the phone to call, then hung up. I needed some courage. I ran across the street and got a six-pack. I also needed a name, just like Dirty Greg. I sat and thought for a minute and drank my beer. Two beers in, I started calling people, beginning with Rosy from Texas.

"What's happening, Rosy? It's Kinky Keith! Just checkin' to

see if you need anything!" I said. Rosy asked me to read her the titles. I had never said any of them out loud, especially not to a woman. I stumbled over the first title. She didn't hear me and asked me to read it again. I couldn't believe the names of some of the films I was reading. We had every genre, every fetish, and every option for every fantasy. It didn't take long before I became immune to the words I was saying because the next thing I knew, I was selling like crazy.

The next morning Greg walked in and saw the stack of orders I had made. It was at least an inch thick. "Wow! You're a salesman! Guess we're gonna hire you a shipper!" And so, we did.

I began organizing the stacks of paper in the office and made company folders and, even though neither of us knew what we were doing, I started doing the bookkeeping and sales. The business grew, and we made money.

Soon we moved from Lancaster to Palmdale because we wanted to grow bigger. We bought a five thousand square foot building and were able to manage it. We sold, shipped, and made money.

Cookie and I followed the store and moved to Palmdale and rented a little house, and while I finally had a job, my resources only made my addiction worse.

Cookie was in a car wreck soon after we moved to Lancaster; she was pregnant, and we got five thousand dollars. I thought I was rich! We bought a car, and I was up to at least a twelve-pack a day, and still did drugs. Cookie was due to have the baby any day when I walked home from the liquor store. "Where's the car?" she asked as I walked in. I held up the case of beer in my hands. I had sold it to get the money for the beer.

A few days later, Cookie started labor and went to the hospital. I sat in the waiting room. I felt numb and scared and detached. I could hardly care for myself, and I had no idea how I was supposed to care for a baby. But, when she was born, I thought she was the most beautiful thing I'd ever seen. We named her Syanne. I left the hospital and went to the closest bar to celebrate! I passed out cigars, telling everyone I had a baby girl and got drunk to avoid going back to the hospital. I stayed out all night.

We lived in a little apartment next to the fairgrounds; it was disgusting, small, and unfit for our new baby. I would sit in the living room and pluck cockroaches off the wall and feed them to the fish in the little tank next to the couch. I listened to Syanne cry and felt annoyed and helpless. As she got a little older, I put on *The Little Mermaid*, her favorite movie, so I could do drugs. When Christmas came around, I bought her a bunch of presents and then took them all back the next day. I wanted to love her, but I was incapable of the selfless love it takes to be a parent, and my inadequacy gave me another reason to want to escape.

Cookie soon got pregnant again. The night she went into labor, she came out in the living room and said, "My water just broke." I was watching porn and tweaking and said, "You better call your sister! I can't do nothing about it!"

When I got up around noon the next day I called over to the hospital. I found out we had another girl. Her name was Sahvon. After Sahvon was born, we both started partying pretty hard, tweaking on meth and dope and not taking care of our girls.

I was a terrible father and a terrible husband, and the guilt was so overwhelming that I fell deeper and deeper into my addiction, and farther and farther away from reality. We had a dog that lay in our front yard and whined every night because it was so hungry; it howled all night hoping for some food or water, but I couldn't even give that to my own kids. I left them alone in their crib and ran to the store to get beer, and come home to find that one of them had jumped out and fallen on her head and was screaming.

Looking for a high one night, I called my dealer, but I had no money. When he got there, I had put for sale signs on everything I owned, willing to trade anything for drugs. When my wife woke up the next morning, everything was gone. I sold the fridge, the pictures off the wall, her wedding rings, the crib our girls slept in. "Where's all our stuff?" she yelled at me. "I sold it," I said matter-of-factly, like it made perfect sense in my stoned mind.

Cookie and I became paranoid, and our addict minds could no longer process what was real. One afternoon she found a picture of a baby boy on the street, and she picked it up and put it in a locket around her neck. She became convinced that it was her baby and we had actually had twins, and the hospital only sent us home with one baby instead of two. Neurotic and frantic, she convinced me to drive down to Beverly Hills to meet with an attorney to sue the hospital.

I called my father looking for sympathy and money and to tell him what the hospital had done. While I had him on the phone, I also told him about how the US was being invaded by the Germans. Very worried for my children, my father called social services and told them they needed to come and get our girls.

I wasn't home when the police showed up but came by the house to see the squad car in the driveway. Cookie was frantic, trying to explain her love for the girls while at the same time telling them that the hospital had stolen her son. The police were putting the girls in the back of the car when I came home, and I watched as they drove away.

We knew that would be the last night in our house, and we spent it getting high. We had two songs together: Linda Ronstadt's "Somewhere Out There" and Barry White's "Just the Way

You Are." While we sat there using, they came on the radio back-to-back. We knew it was our last night together, and we looked at each other in sadness and brokenness, with no hope.

The next morning, the sheriff came by with the landlord and locked the front door with everything in it. As we watched them thread the chains around the handle, all I could think about was following Cookie to the store to get half of her welfare check so I could go get meth. As soon as we split the money, we parted ways. I had lost everything, again. I lost my wife, lost my family, and lost everything I owned, and everything I loved, or tried to love, was gone.

I moved back to Lancaster and started renting a trailer. I was still working for Greg, but only coming into work when I felt like it or wasn't too wasted. I knew he wanted to fire me, but I could come in, after being up all night doing meth, and sell so much that he couldn't let me go. He got so angry with me because I refused to get clean, but his anger subsided when I walked out of the warehouse after a day alone in my office on the phone, and handed him a stack of orders. Nobody could sell like me, and he knew it. Even though I wasn't winning any awards for employee of the month, he still kept me around, whenever I wanted to be.

Soon, the job got in the way of my using. I knew Greg was going to fire me, but I quit before he could. I walked in one day, sold another stack of orders, slammed them on his desk, and said, "I quit."

My life was a wreck, and the paranoia from taking meth continued. I covered my TVs with blankets, thinking they could see me, and I took out the light bulbs from the ceiling because I thought someone was looking at me through the bulb.

After passing out one night in my trailer, I woke up and felt a hot, intense sensation on my back and legs. In my stupor, I looked over to the side of my bed to find a hole on the side of my mattress. It was on fire. I was too wasted to get up, but I knew I had to do something, so I just chucked the mattress outside the back door of the trailer and went back to sleep.

The next morning, I heard rain on my trailer and looked outside my window. Everything was foggy, but there was neither rain or fog outside. It was my hungover brain causing the fog and the water from the hose of a fire truck that I thought was rain. They were putting out a fire on my 1964 Mustang, which was underneath my burning mattress.

I hadn't paid rent in months, and my trailer was loaded with drugs. I grabbed all my stuff, put it in a basket, took a tent, and walked about a block down the alley next to a trailer. I set my tent up in the back of someone's house—a nice family who didn't speak English, and when they came to kick me out, I just looked up at them like it was totally normal that I was there. "Don't worry," I said, "I'm harmless. I just have nowhere to live, so I'm gonna live here." For some reason, they let me stay. The guy next door let me come and get a glass of water, so I could do drugs. He handed me the cup and said, "Just don't break into my house."

I sat on the curb staring at the asphalt. I had heard that Cookie was seeing a guy she'd met in Narcotics Anonymous. I had monitored visits that I kept with my girls, but every time I went I couldn't even speak; I had this baseball-sized knot in my throat. I knew I was a pathetic father and a pathetic human being; I hated everything and everyone around me, and most of all, I hated me.

chapter six

SAMANTHA

I had no driver's license, no wallet, and no key to anything. I had no car, no identification, and no place to live. I had twenty-two cavities in my mouth from the meth and was losing a dangerous amount of weight and becoming malnourished; worst of all, I had no dope, and no dope meant no hope: I was hopeless and dopeless.

A cop drove by as I sat in my tent one day, and he looked inside,"What's going on here, buddy?" "I live here," I told him. And he looked around, got in his squad car, and just left. I was so irate; didn't he want to help me? Take me to jail? DO something?

I decided that it was time to take my problem to somebody who cared; I needed to take it straight to the top. So, the next day, I called city hall. A nice lady answered the phone offering to direct my call. "Yeah, I want to see the mayor," I said. She was direct in her reply, "Sir, you're going to have to have an appointment to do that."

She couldn't schedule me for another two weeks, but that was okay because I had nothing else to do. I counted down each day before my appointment, and when it finally arrived, I grabbed my duffle bag and went into the bathroom at City Hall. I splashed some water on my face and hair. I weighed about 120 pounds and was wearing bailing wire through the loops of my size twenty-eight pants to keep them from falling down.

They brought me a cup of coffee as I waited. The mug had a picture of a Stealth Bomber on in with the words Lockheed Martin written underneath. It felt warm in my hands. I waited a long time until his assistant finally came out and said, "He'll see you now."

Mayor Henry Hearns sat behind his desk. He was larger than life, wearing a pin on his lapel that read "Lancaster City Hall." When I sat down in his office, I knew exactly what I wanted to say even though I didn't even know exactly what I needed. I just knew I needed help. I told him I was an addict and that I lived in an alley and was homeless. "I live in your streets, and I need you to do something to help me," I told him.

He said, "What do you want? A bus ticket out of town?" They would often provide a bus ticket for people in my situation, so they could go back home where they had family and could be someone else's problem.

That's not what I wanted, and at that moment I knew so clearly what I did. I reached into my long green duffle bag and I pulled out two pictures in a frame of my two little girls that were now three and five. I put them up on the desk and said, "No, I want to be a father, and I don't want to be on drugs. But I don't know how to be a father, and I don't know how to get off drugs."

And for the first time, I realized that I meant it. I was at rock bottom; I was ready to get well. For my girls, and for me. I know he must have seen some sincerity in my eyes because he told me to sit and wait in the hallway, and if I was still there at the end of the day, he would help me.

I sat and waited for hours, but I had nowhere to go. I sat on the carpet floor outside his office with my back against the wall until he finally came out around five o'clock. We got in his car, and he drove me to a rough part of town, telling me he pulled some strings to get my first month's rent covered at a recovery house that he knew and trusted. When he dropped me off, he reached into his pocket and gave me a little money, and that was enough to buy a loaf of bread and a dozen eggs.

When I first arrived at the house and started kicking dope, the sweats and nightmares were terrible. I would wake up and walk to a place called, "The Hole in the Wall" and go to these meetings every morning, noon, and night. They weren't very populated meetings. People showed up drunk and fell asleep on the floor. It was my first introduction to a twelve-step program, and showing up there kept me clean.

I remember being so happy. I was making progress. I was going somewhere. I had strength. I had hope.

And soon, I also had one year clean! I called Mayor Henry Hearns and asked him if he would come give me my cake. I told all my friends from my program that I had a big surprise for them. The room was crowded when the mayor of Lancaster walked in the door, wearing the same suit and official pin on his lapel. He gave me my cake and told the story of how we'd met, how I asked him for help and how proud he was that I had gotten clean. I reached into my pocket and paid him back the money he had given me to get started on this new journey.

One afternoon I was walking down the Sierra Highway and suddenly, a Rolls-Royce whooshed to a stop in front of me. The driver rolled down the window, and I looked inside. It was Greg. The cold air-conditioning seemed to leap out of the car and felt so good on my face that was being scorched in the hot desert sun.

"What are you doing?" he asked, with a slight mixture of pity and sarcasm.

"I got clean, and I live in the recovery house up the way," I said.

"Get in!" he said.

"Well, I got nothing else to do," I said.

And there it was. That moment stepping into that car was a step into a life. He offered me a job again, right then and there, and he told me I could work in the warehouse. He told me I wasn't allowed to do sales until he was sure I was actually clean, but it didn't take long after I started for him to put me back on the phones.

His company had grown in the time I had been away. He had started selling sex toys and was up to five salespeople now, and life became easy. I had a well of money that other people in my world didn't have; I was making sixty grand a year, and things were good.

I was renting a room from a guy named "Burnt Paul," and I would take the city bus to go see my girls. They were three and five and living with their aunt. During my visits she stared at me with disgust when I was there, but I didn't give up on them. They were the reason I had come this far, and I was going to keep showing up.

Not long after, Cookie finally got custody back; she had been working hard for a year to bring them home, and once she did, I got a place two streets over from her so I could see my girls more often. I even went to the DMV and got a state ID. I remember going out and buying a wallet and getting a key made for my apartment. I was so happy and proud to have an ID and a key. I continued going to meetings and bought a car, even though I didn't have a license to drive it, and then I met a girl.

I met her at a recovery meeting and thought she was beautiful, and I began driving to meetings to try and find her. It was just another good reason to go to meetings. She drove a jeep, and I looked for her jeep, and if I didn't see it, I went to another meeting.

She worked at Denny's, and I would show up and sit in her station and watch her. She could go up to a table of twenty people and take everyone's order and not write one thing down. She would come back and set everyone's plate in front of them and not miss one thing. I thought she was incredible.

I learned that she liked elephants, and I bought her a necklace with two elephants that had their trunks tied together and gave it to her. She looked at me like I was a weirdo and walked away, but she kept the necklace, so I figured there was hope, but she didn't make it easy.

Playing hard to get, she danced around my affections, always keeping me intrigued enough to stick around but never willing to commit to anything. We went out a few times, but it was nothing serious. I really liked her. I told my friend I liked her. "You know what you gotta do," my friend said, "take out her best friend … then it'll make her jealous and she'll want to go out with you!" That seemed like great advice to me, and so I called her friend Tammy, and we hung out all night. The next morning, I let Tammy borrow my car and walked over to Denny's and sat in the section I always did—hers.

She walked over and asked suspiciously, "Where's your car?"

"Tammy has it," I said.

I told her it was because Tammy had spent the night and wanted to borrow it. "I thought you weren't interested, so I decided to start seeing other people," I told her.

"Go get your car," she said.

"Hold on," I said, "if I go get my car, does that mean you're ready to commit?"

"Yes," she said, "just go get your car from that girl." And that was the beginning of my life with her and the end of any other girl. Her name was Samantha, and we were madly in love. We dated for about a year and then, on a whim one weekend, we decided to drive to Vegas and get married.

We drove to the Luxor Hotel and had our honeymoon the night before we got married. We booked a room on our drive, and when we arrived, the room they gave us had two full beds and a slanted ceiling. I marched down to the front desk and said, "This room won't do. We are on our honeymoon, and this is no way to start out a happy marriage." They quickly gave me another room—a massive suite, which would end up being our first of many massive suites in Vegas; we just didn't know it yet. We felt rich and famous. We drank sparkling cider from pyramid wine glasses, and the next morning we drove to a little white chapel and got married. I had a mullet, Samantha had a perm, and we were so nervous that we laughed through the whole ceremony.

On our way home Greg called and yelled at me for missing a day of work. I was excited to tell him the news, "Can't I take a day off to get married?" He said no. I felt both angry at his dependence and satisfied that I was the hero of the place. They could hardly last a day without me, but he didn't care if I got married; he wanted me there selling.

chapter seven

KING KEITH

Now that I had a new wife, and we were on the journey of sobriety together, what I wanted was what I'd always wanted: a home. Greg came to me one day with an offer to buy a house that he was upside-down on, and we assumed the loan. I used to drive to work and see houses like the one we were about to buy and wonder how people would ever be able to buy a home, and here I was, a homeowner.

We soon took out a second loan and put in a pool and hot tub; I have so many good memories of that place, especially of my girls coming over and swimming and splashing in the backyard. The house was on a cul-de-sac, and while it came with 1,400 square feet and a garage, it also came with a lot of stigma. All the neighbors on the street seemed to know enough about Greg, because of his gold chains and Cadillac and place of work, that if we knew him they didn't want to know us. And though we owned our home, we were still missing what I hoped would come with it: a community. But most of our neighbors kept to themselves.

Business was starting to boom like never before, and we were thriving; I could see potential for us to grow, and Greg and I motivated each other with a unique synergy of competition and comradery. We started pulling in around four million a year, and I loved watching what we built grow, but one day it occurred to me that no matter how much the company was making, I was still making the same sixty thousand dollar salary, and I was starting to get fed up and resentful.

I had a relationship with one of the producers from an adult film company called Devil's Films. He always told me I was the star of our business and said that if I ever wanted to go into business on my own that all it would take was one phone call, but I had always been loyal to Greg. I always planned to be loyal to the end—party together, work together, do life together. He was my only friend, but now that I was sober, I was starting to see things more clearly and realized I was headed toward a dead end.

I had always thought I wasn't worth much, but I was good at this—good at selling, good at creating, and good at building. I convinced myself that maybe I would be good enough on my own, without Greg. I called the Devil's Films producer and drove to meet him in the Valley. He told me that he would be willing to be my silent partner if I went out on my own as a distributor of films, but I was sworn to secrecy. It would be scandalous for a producer to partner with a single distributor, so we agreed to silence. When I got home, I was busting at the seams with the excitement of the possibility as well as the sheer terror of having to prove myself, but I had Samantha, and she was smart, so I felt like, with her, I could do anything. And we got to work.

We found an old shotgun building in Santa Clarita by Magic Mountain and rented it. With the bankroll of our silent partner, we spent every spare minute in that empty building getting it ready. We hired someone to build shelves for product, incorporated the company, bought new cell phones to replace the phone Greg made us pay for, bought new computers (even though I'd never stroked a keyboard in my life) and got things set up for our big exit from Greg. My friend Donny and I left the warehouse in a very Jerry-Maguire-esque moment, but Greg wasn't even there to see it; we said our goodbyes, grabbed our stuff, and left.

And just like that, my days with Greg were over, and our days at Premier Sales Group began. We started making calls that night, without a moment to lose, calling manufacturers to order product. By that night, Greg heard about my exit and was blowing up my phone trying to reach me. I refused to answer; I was on my new phone trying to get clients.

Greg wasted no time either; he called at least fifty different manufactures and told them I stole from him to start this new company. He couldn't figure out how I had the capital to go out on my own. He told them I had backed up a truck in the night and taken everything from him. He called all my loyal customers, and I was blacklisted. My biggest customer even sent Greg a dozen black roses with a card that read, "In memory of Keith." No one would sell to me. They supported Greg.

Desperate for revenge, Greg pressed charges for theft and corporate espionage, for stealing product and secrets from his company to start my own. Both charges ended up getting dismissed because of the monotonous and expensive work the court ordered, and there was nothing there. My attorney informed him that if he didn't drop the case, we would countersue for harassment. So he dropped the case, but he didn't leave me alone.

I had to get out of his old house, people were telling me that he had hired private investigators to watch me and that he was at my house when I wasn't, so we sold our home for a thirty thousand dollar profit and moved to Santa Clarita.

I remember walking into the bank with thirty thousand dollars cash in my hand. I wanted to walk around and wave it in front of every teller at his or her window. I wanted a flood of people to wait on me and try and earn the thousands I was bringing them. I had arrived, and I was bigtime. I walked up to a teller with a new attitude: *Serve me.* I didn't actually say that, but I thought it and acted like it. I was finally what I had aspired to be, a combination of my heroes: my dad and my boss—the playboy, bookie, fireman, gambler, married-six-times kind of guy. I was on the road I wanted to be: more prestige, more cash, more cars, more respect … more of it all. I was mafia. I was gangster. I was thug. Except I wasn't, really, but in that moment, you could have fooled me.

Once I opened that account, Samantha and I rented a house in Santa Clarita, in Canyon Country, and this was my first time out of Palmdale since I'd hitched that ride from Memphis. We were proud of ourselves and going to work to keep it that way.

Getting the company up and running started slow. We still couldn't buy direct. Samantha, Donny, and I would call and call, but the phones were dead for hours while we waited for someone, anyone, to return a call.

Eventually, I decided that we needed to run an ad in a magazine, and if we were going to do it, we were gonna go big. I thought, *If they're not going to give me attention, I'm going to demand it.* So, I took out a full page ad with a picture of me, Magnum PI mustache and all, with a crown on my head and text that read, "Discount Whore of the Industry. My prices can't be beat. Call me King Keith."

The calls started flooding in. Sales began to climb. We rented another building, hired shippers, and began building and improving our inventory. I gave each and every customer all the attention I had. I knew that if I invested in friendships, I would keep them around.

I remember a client named Robert from Kilgore, Texas, who called me one night because he was thinking about opening up a store. We sat on the phone for three hours, and I told him all about the business. He ended up opening that store and six more and became one of my biggest, most loyal customers.

One time he came to visit, and I bought him a nice room with a suite, loaned him a car, took him to dinner, and then to my warehouse. His first response at seeing this place we had worked so hard to build was, "I thought it would be bigger." It shot me through the heart, and that night I went out and rented another shotgun building that was ten thousand square feet. I took him over there the next morning and said, "How's this?"

I was still being dared to prove myself, and even though we struggled, we kept growing. People started hearing about us, and even people that didn't want to sell to me because of my bad blood with Greg were selling to me. Samantha was brilliant. She made cold calls and called everyone in the area and worked for hours, just trying again and again.

I remember her calling one store in Texas. I could tell in her voice that it was a big order, and I mouthed to her, "How much?" She wrote, "10,000!" She quickly became our best salesperson, outselling Donny and me.

There was a rush to it all. We were building and making something out of nothing, and soon after moving to our new building, we tripled our space. It was all happening so quickly. One afternoon, I took an order from Hawaii for a quarter million dollars. As I was on the phone, our forklift broke in the middle of loading one of our trucks. I yelled down to the guys, "Don't worry about it!" And the next day there was a forty thousand dollar forklift delivered to our door.

My money was doubled. I was taking good quarterly bonuses, and the world was serving us. UPS and FedEx started battling for our business; we had two eighteen-wheel trucks coming through daily, and we were filling them up. But one thing I've learned about money is that as soon as you get some, you want more.

We were soaring and so was our potential, plus we'd always loved to gamble—and the rush of our success made us hungry for more, so when my silent partner from Devil's Films called me and asked if I'd want to buy him out of his production company, even though I didn't even really know exactly what it was or what it did, I just said, "What's it make?" He told me it pulled in a couple million a year. I asked what he wanted for it. "A year's pay," was his answer. "All right! Got nothing else to do!" I joked.

We eventually bought out the production company, and it was a whole new animal. I didn't know anything about production, but I was a businessman, and Samantha could make whatever she touched better. She paid attention to colors and did everything with intentionality and excellence. We started moving everything from analogue to high definition. People started noticing our products and liked us. They wanted to do business with us, and we kept growing and growing. We paid off the company in a year and tripled its revenue.

I remembered that when I was a kid, my dad used to tell me to save my money, and I called home when all this was happening, and my dad asked me if I was saving my money. I said, "Dad, I'm making so much I can't help but save it!" It was coming at us so fast, and we couldn't spend it as fast as we made it.

We had enough money now to upgrade to a new house, and

as we were driving through the beautiful homes in Agua Dulce, Samantha told me that she wanted to buy one. There is something deep and instinctual that happens when your lady wants something; whether or not it makes sense, you want to provide it for her. I didn't think I'd be able to figure it out; my credit was shot because of back child support and outstanding ambulance bills from back in my partying days. Regardless, I got a loan and paid $436,000 for a house in Agua Dulce.

Things just kept getting bigger and better; life just kept dealing out Aces, and we were hitting "Blackjack!" everywhere we went. At least that's what it seemed like on the outside, but the truth was, even though we were making more money than ever before, we were lacking what we wanted the most, we just didn't know what it was. We kept trying to fill our lives with everything we could find to fill our hearts, but nothing would satisfy. We had each other, but we were still lonely, still looking, and still felt isolated from the rest of the world.

It seemed like everywhere we went, everyone knew what we did; we didn't know how, but somehow they found out. Once we bought our girls a pink electric golf cart with zebra seats and mag wheels and a banging stereo. They rode around the neighborhood, with Madonna's "Material Girl" blaring. One afternoon, as our daughters cruised past our home with a neighbor, the neighbor girl piped up from the back of the cart, "You know what those people do for work?" Our daughter pretended that it wasn't her house. "What?" she said, sheepishly. "They make porn," the little girl whispered.

Our daughter came home and told us what had happened. They always sort of knew what we did, but we never took them to work or brought our work home. We didn't want them around it, but it still kept the community from wanting to be around us.

Every time I got a glimpse of what it would be like to have friend-ships or be in community, I got burned, and all I learned from my community was that I needed to hide.

We decided to try another neighborhood, so I sold that $436,000 house for $1.125 million. The morning of our moving day, we woke up to graphic graffiti drawn all over the street in front of our home and crude words sprawling across the concrete to say goodbye. We felt so humiliated.

We moved to a home in Canyon Country in a fairly average neighborhood, and even though I paid around $700,000 for the house, it didn't meet my expectations. We spent weeks updating the house. We had Bentleys and hot rods; I couldn't even fit all of my cars in the garage, and I was dripping with jewelry and watches and expensive clothes.

It was clear that we did something to be able to afford the house, the cars, the watches, the jewelry, and the toys, but when anyone would ask what I did for a living, my response was the same: "As little as possible." That always got a laugh but also left them curious.

We lived between a school principal and a cop, and the cop would scale my fence, trying to figure out what I was hiding. I'm sure he was convinced that I was drug dealer, or maybe a rapper. I don't know. When I think about my mullet at the time, probably not a rapper.

But I was getting bored again. The search for a home con-tinued, even though we had lived in so many nice houses. One afternoon I saw a house that had a pool that overlooked the eigh-teenth hole of a golf course. It cost two million dollars, and it wasn't far from the house we just moved into. I told Samantha, "I want this house. This one is gonna make me happy."

She wanted to get my mind off it; we had just moved, so she

made another suggestion: "What if we bought a little beach house? Let's go look in Ventura and see if we can find anything." So we drove out to the little beach community about forty-five miles away. It was a sunny eighty degrees, and we looked at four houses and made an offer on the fourth that afternoon.

The owner countered, and we accepted. A friend of mine now, he told me that they weren't sure we were serious until they went to check the mailbox a couple days later and found a receipt for all the furniture we had ordered to be delivered. He called his wife and told her about the receipt, "I guess they bought the house!"

chapter eight

YOGURT

Samantha and I had been sober for twelve years when we purchased that little weekend place in Ventura. We started feeling less and less responsibility with the business; it was basically running itself now, and my daughters were graduating from high school. We had a lot of freedom, living back and forth between Santa Clarita and Ventura.

That's when we started dabbling a little more with drugs and alcohol. I started telling myself I could handle it, that I was better now and all grown up. I could smoke a little weed, have a drink or two, take a pill, take a hit, and it wouldn't bother me. Someone gave me pills down at the beach one day, and it was like I found God. I could drink all night on them, so I loved life down on the beach.

Soon, our weekend home became more like our monthly home. My kids were living by themselves up in Canyon Country and coming down on the weekends when I wasn't messed up. I enjoyed my freedom. It was nice. People in Ventura weren't always looking at what kind of car you were driving or how good your grass looked. They didn't care about what kind of purse you were carrying or watch you were wearing; they weren't impressed with people trying to impress.

It was refreshing, and I told Samantha that we needed to move there permanently, but the house we bought was too small. I drove around Ventura looking for a bigger place and found one in the Hills that I liked. I thought it looked like the nicest house in Ventura, but it wasn't for sale. I had our Realtor knock on the door and make an offer, and the owners agreed, but when I went to look at it, I changed my mind because the inside didn't match the outside. How ironic that I rejected it because it was basically a reflection of my life.

Instead, I found a duplex for sale by owner on one of the lanes leading to the beach. I told him I'd buy it and paid $900,000 for it, in cash. We quickly tore it down and built our dream home. This was where we would finally arrive, finally be happy, and finally be home.

But something was still missing, and Sam decided she wanted to have a baby. Over the years we had tried to have a baby, but we weren't able to conceive. We had tried some other routes: in vitro, surrogacy—nothing ever worked. We eventually adopted the baby of an old friend of a friend, despite our background with drugs and alcohol and our current occupation.

We went to the hospital the night our son, Jaxon, was born, and Samantha was in the delivery room with the mother. We were now living in a neighborhood in Ventura called Pierpont, getting used to being parents again, and one of Samantha's favorite things to do was to get frozen yogurt. We kept talking about how our neighborhood needed its own yogurt shop.

There was a little fruit stand on the corner of Pierpont and Seward, right as you pulled off the exit on Highway 101. It was the perfect spot. I had met and become friends with the woman who owned it, and one day, she asked me if I wanted to buy it. I went home and told Samantha, and we decided to do it—another adventure for the books. And so there we were: a dream home, a new yogurt shop, and a new son. Life was looking really good.

We tried to learn everything we could about yogurt, since we really knew nothing except that we liked to eat it. We went to another yogurt shop and looked at their machines and saw the name, "Taylor." I googled it, and it said they had a convention in Las Vegas that week, so we decided to drop what we were doing and go.

The yogurt convention was at the same place as an electronics convention that we went to each year. We would set up a booth in the adult show area, and I never waited in any lines and always had an entourage. Then, I was King Keith. Here, I was nobody. I even had to buy a badge.

That next week, a representative from Taylor came and looked at our shop. She took one look at our tiny 390 square foot building and her first words were, "You didn't rent this did you?" As she began to list all the things we were going to have to try and fit in that space to get it up to code (a three compartment sink, a vegetable sink, a mop sink, a bigger hot water heater, a wheelchair accessible bathroom, a prep bar, a food bar, and a three compartment refrigerator), she told me it would never work. That was just the challenge I needed.

As soon as she left, I was on the phone with an architect and told him to draw it up. There wasn't a lot of life on that corner, just two liquor stores directly across from each other and a lot of homeless people camped out in-between. It wasn't somewhere people wanted to send their kids or hang around, but I envisioned families walking there after school with their dogs, kids setting up ramps and skateboarding in the parking lot, and teenagers finding an excuse to stop by with their friends on their way home. I wanted to bring a little good, a little life to this forgotten space; it felt like I was finally doing something different. Something I didn't have to hide from my neighbors. Something I didn't feel shame about. Something that was even redeeming to that little corner.

I printed large banners to announce our opening, and just as we were getting things off and running, I got a phone call from my friend Alby (we all call him Donut). "Hey, you might want to come down here. Something has happened to your sign," he said.

I jumped on my bicycle and rode over. There it was in bright red paint on the front window of the store: "PORN STARS WANTED." Over my banner it said, "PORN PRODUCERS."

I was devastated. I was so ashamed. The secret was out. I started to wonder how many people had already seen it. The damage was done. Everyone knew. I was sure they were all talking and spreading false rumors about how I was using the shop to wash my money from my porn business; it was devastating.

I dreaded telling Samantha. I felt so defeated, and all I could think of was how we were going to have to move again. Leave. Get out of this place. Who was I kidding that I could just start over like this? Just because I had a new house, new cars, new stuff, a new son ... how did I think that would make a new me?

But Samantha is stronger than me and this resistance just made her want to dig her heels in deeper. "We're not going anywhere," she said. She wanted to get on our bicycles and ride down Pierpont with our heads held high. I thought she was crazy, but she has a way of pushing me out of myself.

Now, whenever I meet a person with a hard exterior, I remember that moment and how I'd spent a lifetime creating walls around me that I was determined to turn into a fortress—all the while I was so weak and just dying inside. I was so lonely and afraid. I was trying to make a round peg fit into a square hole. This store was a bandage on an open, gaping wound. I was at the gym and doing steroids trying to look good, and I was wearing expensive watches trying to look good, but something was so broken, so missing.

It's always interesting to me how there can be a physical representation on the outside of something much deeper. It was time to build some walls. I had security cameras installed and a chain link fence placed around my little building. I also hung a new banner, this one with a little more ferocity: "Surf 'n Yogurt, Coming Soon;" it was all I could do not to add "like it or not."

The night before our grand opening, everything was done. We stood outside, offering free tasters to people riding their bikes on the bike path or people strolling to the beach, and we invited them to come back the next day. I had decided to buy five hundred bright red T-shirts with "Surf 'n Yogurt" written in big letters across the front in youth and adult sizes, and I would tell kids that if they came back the next day they got a free shirt.

All day there was a stream of people, and even though we weren't open, there seemed to be a buzz. There was this one guy and his son who stopped by. They had a little Shar-Pei puppy, and the father stood out to me in the crowd because he seemed like an alien. Like he was inhumanly happy. He greeted me with such a lively spirit and big smile that I was like, *What's wrong with this guy?* I told him we weren't open yet, but I gave him a free cup of yogurt, and he told me that his name was Jude Fouquier and that his wife loved yogurt and was excited about this shop opening on the corner. I wasn't sure about them as they left, but they made an impression on my wife and me. I was hoping they weren't the only ones excited about the new yogurt in the neighborhood.

We went home that night and barely slept. We were so nervous and sure nobody would show up the next day. We talked about how embarrassing it was going to be to have dumped all this money into this little shop, and the word was out about what we did for a living; we thought no one would want to come. I leaned over to Samatha just as we started to fall asleep and said, "If we can just survive winter, at least we'll make money in the summertime when the tourists are in town and don't know what we do for a living." It wasn't funny, but we laughed.

The next morning, we went down and we opened the door, and a few people trickled in. We fiddled around, arranging things and just trying to look busy; it was slower than we wanted, but two blocks away there was a little elementary school on the beach that had heard we were open for business, and word had spread about our free T-shirts. By 2:15 p.m., we had a line around the store, and the parking lot was full of people. We hadn't planned it, but our opening day was also the Open House night at that little, local elementary school.

For the first time in our lives we were finding connections with people from our neighborhood; we were meeting teachers, principals, cops, park rangers, and firefighters. Sometimes they would just pull up in their fire truck and hop out to get a cup of yogurt. I was talking to all the people I had avoided for so long—all the people I assumed would judge me when they found out what I did for a living. I guess they hadn't seen the banner.

It was a great success, and for a while it felt great, but something was still missing. I still wasn't happy. I had the store, and once again I had made it, done it, and achieved success. Still, I suffered from just being me.

chapter nine

REAL LIFE

One afternoon when I was working at the store that alien-looking guy, Jude, showed up again. He still had the sparkle in his eyes as he came in to get a cup of yogurt. I don't know what happened to me in that moment, but I felt compelled to ask him if maybe we could meet for coffee. "Heck yeah!" was his answer, and we set a date for the Starbucks around the corner from my shop.

When we sat down at a little two-seater in the middle of the store, I was so uncomfortable. It got worse. Jude told me he had moved to Ventura from Seattle to start a new church called City Church and that he was a pastor. I didn't want anything to do with anyone that had any kind of religion, but there was just something about this guy. He was charismatic, full of life, normal, and maybe even said an occasional curse word or two; he almost made it seem like it was OK to love God. That it didn't have to be a bad thing.

I don't know why, but I wanted to tell him the truth about my life, and right then and there, I told him my story. I told him how unhappy I was and how I was really making my money. I expected him to bolt. I expected him to judge—to flip tables and point fingers. But after I was done, he just sat there. I looked at him and said, "Well, what do you think? Do you still like me?" I laughed uncomfortably.

He complimented my laugh, and he said, "Your story doesn't change how I feel about you, but would you mind if I prayed for you?"

I said, "Are you crazy? Right here in this Starbucks in the middle of Pierpont? No way!" There was no way I was going to be seen in public praying with another man. I mean, I know I sold porn for a living, but that was just embarrassing!

I told him that if he really wanted to pray, we could go sit in my car, and I pointed to my attention-getting, twin turbo, AMG, murdered out, and flat black-rimmed Mercedes S65, which he later nicknamed my, "Almighty God Car." As we sat in the car, he prayed for me and had me repeat a prayer after him that I later learned was called "the prayer of salvation."

And he said, "Keith, you just gave your life to Christ. How do you feel about that?" I said, "I don't know how I feel about that. It just happened." And I didn't know. It just happened, and it happened fast, and yet, there was something about this moment that was like a cracked door opening up, letting light into a dark room. Something about the moment made me trust that it was significant.

Jude asked me a favor. I said maybe. He said, "Would you come to church with me on Sunday?" All I could say was that I would think about it. But what surprised me was that I actually meant it. I came home and told Samantha that I thought I might go to church on Sunday. Her response went something like, "WHAT?!" But I told her about meeting that guy from the yogurt shop and how I wanted to check out his church.

She was pretty sure I had lost my mind, but figured it was just going to be one of my many phases. Like any addict, I loved to try new things and go all in, until I didn't want to anymore. I think she thought it would run its course, just like everything else had.

That Sunday I woke up and decided to actually go. Samantha didn't want to go with me. I left her and my son behind, and I pulled into the back of the parking lot. I looked through the cars to the front doors, and now every person I saw looked like an alien. They all had that same smile, the same weird twinkling eyes, and I figured it was probably a cult.

It was so hard for me to open that door and put my foot onto the ground of that parking lot. I sat there for a long time, trying so hard to leave but something made me want to stay. *What if there is something here? What if there's answers, what if there's hope, and what if there's a different way?* I thought. I just wanted something different so badly.

I stepped out of the car and began walking toward the crowd of strange people standing at the doors. They were nice, but I was scared. And there was that guy again. "Hey Keith!" Jude yelled across the crowd. He welcomed me in with open arms and said, "Come on in here!"

The first person he introduced me to was a guy named Mike. I learned later on that Mike was one of the wealthier people in his church, but when Jude introduced me he said, "This is Mike; he used to sell drugs! We call him Marijuana Mike!" And all I could think was, *Oh my gosh, he's gonna introduce me as the guy who used to sell porn, and they're gonna call me Porno Keith!*

But he never did. He let my secret stay safe, and Mike let me sit by him toward the back. When the band came out, the music was like something I'd never heard before. It was nothing like what I remembered as a kid—that melancholy hum that bored me to death and didn't sound like anything else on the radio. This music was new and fun and people were having a good time and engaged, both young and old, jumping around, singing, dancing, and having a blast.

What is this place? I thought as my new friend Jude took the stage and began to speak. His message grabbed ahold of me. I understood what he was talking about and it resonated with me on a whole new level, in a whole new place in my heart. I went home and told Samantha how much I loved it—and told her she should come with me. She told me she would never go and to leave her alone, but I had to go back.

For six months I attended by myself, and this newfound faith was changing me. It was making sense and filling a void in me that had never come close to being filled before. I longed to talk about it and to share it with Samantha, but she was resistant. She had never been to church, never had a faith in God, and didn't trust what was happening to me.

Samatha had a younger brother named Drew, who lived in Santa Clarita and was dating a girl named Deanna who had become a Christian a year or two before. We all thought she caught a disease. Her newfound faith was so strange. She talked differently, acted differently, and went to church all the time. We made fun of her and rolled our eyes when she talked about her faith, and I think Samantha couldn't imagine me becoming the same. Jude encouraged me to just pray for her and give her time, so I did.

Deanna had gotten involved in a church in Santa Clarita called Real Life. She faithfully attended every week, and even dragged Drew there with her sometimes. One Sunday, the church announced that it was planting a new church in Ventura, and Deanna's heart leaped. Young as she was in her faith, it was her primary passion that her boyfriend's family would grow to love

God. God had rescued her out of the porn industry and changed her life, and she longed for us to experience the same.

She instantly began to believe that this new church would play a role in reaching our family. She even asked God to allow one of the team members from the planting team to live on Pierpont. One Sunday, Real Life's pastor mentioned the church again and said if anyone wanted to meet the team that they would be hanging out in the coffee shop after the service.

Deanna brought Drew and introduced herself to one of the team members, Jodi Hickerson, and told her about us. "I have family who own a yogurt shop on Pierpont called Surf 'n Yogurt, have you heard of it?" he asked.

Jodi laughed, and said, "I need to introduce you to my friend Jen—that Surf 'n Yogurt is Jen's favorite place." When Deanna came over to Jen, she mentioned the yogurt shop and told her about us. Instantly, Jen's eyes filled with tears. She told Deanna the miracle of how she and her family had ended up renting on Pierpont and for the last several months had been praying for the owners of that yogurt shop. She didn't know our story, only that they had moved to the area to be missionaries to their city, and she and her kids loved yogurt. As a family, they decided to pray for the owners of the neighborhood shop they were at so often.

By the end of the conversation, both girls were teary-eyed as Deanna said, "We need to meet. I need to tell you my story."

Deanna was once one of the most recognized and famous porn stars in the industry but was an addict and broken. She had hit a low point when a fan of hers left his wife and came to a show to meet her, hoping for a relationship; when he was denied, he went home and shot himself. Deanna learned of this tragedy through a letter sent to her from his wife. Deanna overdosed on alcohol at a party, and it was her boyfriend, Drew, who came alongside her after that incident and was instrumental in getting her clean and helping her escape the industry.

After sharing her story and her loyalty to this family she loved so much, she mentioned that Samantha, being new to the area, might like a friend and that Jen should give her a call. So one day, Samantha got a text from this random girl on her phone, introducing herself as a friend of Deanna's, and she asked Samantha if she might like to go for a walk or something sometime.

Now, this was something Samantha would never do; in fact, she thought it sounded crazy, but for some reason, she said yes, and she and this girl Jen met up to go on a walk. Both competitive in nature, they started to walk and kept waiting for the other person to suggest turning around. They ended up walking several miles that first day, and I was hoping that when they got home, Samantha would have had the same experience I had with Jude, but it wasn't like that at all.

They didn't talk a whole lot about God or religion or church, but they hit it off instantly, kindred spirits to the core. They started to walk together frequently. Jen just loved Samantha and listened to her where she was at. Over the next few months, they developed a deep friendship, and I watched my wife change. She was more open and excited about having a close friend; she had never really had that before, and it was really special.

Months passed, and we decided it was time to open up a new yogurt shop in a nearby city. On our opening day, Jen and her family came to support us, and we sat and ate yogurt outside our new place. It meant a lot to Samantha that Jen and her family drove over for it, so a couple weeks later, when Jen invited her to the launch of the church, Mission Church, in Ventura, Samantha decided to go.

Samantha told me, "Well, she came to my opening, so I feel

like I should go to hers, but *don't* ask me to go again. I'm just going to go this *one time*."

That morning when we arrived, Jen found us in the lobby and sat with Samantha as Mike Hickerson, the lead pastor, taught on the story of the prodigal son. They were starting a series, and the first week was about the younger brother. During the message, Samantha leaned over to Jen and said, "Is this a true story or where is this story from?" Jen told her that it was a story that Jesus told to try and help people understand the love of God. "This is the most amazing story I've ever heard," Samantha whispered back.

That afternoon, I asked Samantha what she thought, and she said she liked it, but she had to go back the next week and find out what happened to the older brother!

So my wife and I started attending church together, and I was getting so excited about my newfound faith. I remember walking into a Christian bookstore for the first time in my life because I wanted to buy a Bible, but I didn't know they would have so many choices. I called Jude and asked which one to get, and he told me not to get one. The next time I saw him, he had one for me.

I remember sitting in the mall parking lot listening to a CD that Deanna had given me. It was the first Christian music I'd ever owned, and I thought it was the most beautiful music I had ever heard in my life. It overwhelmed me; it was like something inside me was awake, aware, and alive for the first time. I called Jude because the feeling was kind of freaking me out; I felt crazy and told him how I was feeling. He told me that it was the Holy Spirit. I didn't know exactly what that meant, but whenever I was at a stoplight I would pull up next to people and roll down my window and say, "Listen to this! Have you ever heard anything like this before?"

Suddenly, life was exciting. Suddenly it felt like it had meaning, purpose. There was *life* in my life!

I had started over so many times. But this felt different. This felt new. But, there was still so much in my life that didn't feel right. It wasn't like as soon as I said that prayer then, BAM, I changed into a new person instantly, but it was like I understood why in that song "Amazing Grace," they sing, "I was blind, but now I see." It's like scales were starting to fall off my eyes. Now that I had cracked the door to the light, I was starting to see the darkness left in me, and I knew that I couldn't go all in with God until I let go of the porn businesses.

chapter ten

SOLD!

W hen I gave my life to Christ, we were still driving over to Santa Clarita and overseeing all the work being done in the warehouse and with our companies, and I was taking home over 3.2 million dollars a year, with no education, no degree and, honestly, not much effort.

But every time I would go over to Santa Clarita, during that forty-five-minute drive, it felt like my spirit started to ache. God was ruining my experience of going to work. When I arrived at the warehouse, I was miserable. I walked into the building and saw the pictures, read the titles, heard the language, and what used to not faze me at all, bothered me, irritated me, and made me feel uneasy to my core. It reminded me of the beginning days when I walked through the warehouse with Greg and tried to keep my head down because I was so embarrassed by the titles, but it was worse—like suddenly I had a conscience.

It was like when I was in Ventura and at church and with God there was sunshine and warmth all over me, and it felt so right; there was no other feeling like it. But when I went to my business, it was like I was walking out of the light, and I felt a dark cloud come over me, between me and God. All I wanted to do was to get warm again and get back into the light, back into the sunshine of God.

I was trying to live in both worlds, but the darkness and the light couldn't coexist. So, I started going over as little as possible and when I did, I stayed as little as possible. I would show up, smoke one cigar with my employees and say, "Well guys, I gotta go!" And then I turned around and drove back, until I realized it just wasn't worth it anymore. The money, the power, and the success: I would give it all up if it meant I could stay in the light.

I decided that I wanted to get baptized. I had heard people talking about it, and they had said you don't have to be perfect or have it all figured out before you do it. Still, I decided that if I was going to do it, I wanted to get completely out of the industry first. I wanted to come up out of the water and say, "That was my past; I'm done owning those companies, and I'm done with that industry. Figuratively and literally, I'm done with that old life."

It took Samantha and me awhile to get on the same page. It was hard to walk away from that kind of money when we hardly had to do anything, and we had worked so incredibly hard to build what we had. But it was amazing to see our new friends, who were basically all pastors, (which was funny in itself) having patience with us in the process and not requiring us to do anything or change anything before we were loved, accepted, and allowed to be used by God. Jude even encouraged me to wait to sell until Samantha was ready; that I had to be patient with her in her own journey and trust God's timing would lead us both in the same direction.

I started getting opportunities to volunteer at the church and couldn't believe this new life we were starting to live. I felt so unworthy. One day I called Jude, and we met at that same Star-bucks in Pierpont where we had met nine months before when I had accepted Christ in my life. This time, I wrestled with what was next, and if I'd ever be good enough to follow God. I'll never forget Jude's words. He said, "Keith, God knew what he got when he got you."

God knew what he got when he got me. Could that be true? Those words sunk so deep in my soul, like a knife cutting through the hardest parts of me to my very core. This was the kind of love that was changing me. That God could know everything about me and love and want to use me anyway. It blew me away.

I kept becoming new, one day at a time, and it was starting to show. One day at the office, I had a run-in with an old client. There was a mix-up, and he thought I owed him money. I thought I didn't. He sent a big gangster-looking dude who could barely fit through my office door to get it back. I was on the phone when he walked in, and he interrupted me and said, "Jake wants his money."

"I don't owe Jake any money!" I barked back.

"Well, that be your decision," he said, "but don't make me come back."

"You don't have to come back," I yelled after him, "I'm here right now! What do you want to do?" He didn't come back, and I was secretly glad. I wasn't actually sure what I was going to do.

I called in one of my coworkers after he left and told him to take care of it, which meant that he told his people about it, and his people put a hit out on him.

The manager from my other company called and asked, "Did you put a hit on Jake?" And then he warned me, "Those people you called are no joke, but Jake's no joke either!"

I drove back to Ventura that night, and I started thinking about Jake. Thinking about other people besides myself was still new for me. But I started wondering about him—about his life, who he was, what would happen if this all played out, and I just had a strong feeling that what I needed to do was just sit down with him and have a conversation. So, I called Jake and asked him to meet me in the Valley at a Starbucks. He agreed. Who knew it could be that simple? And at Starbucks no less?

The whole way there I prayed, and when I arrived, I glanced around the room, trying to see if there were any other big, suspicious looking people who might want to hurt me. Finally, Jake arrived and sat down. He looked angry and ready for a fight, and I heard myself say, "Listen, I just want to tell you I'm getting out of this business ... I found Jesus and I'm changing my life."

As the words were coming out of my mouth I was thinking, *What am I doing? Where did that come from? Why am I telling this man this?*

But it was the truth; I was headed down a new road. I didn't know why, but I just wanted to tell this guy. I really thought I had lost my mind.

After I finished talking, Jake stared at me for a few seconds that felt like a thousand years, then said, "That is so weird; I just had a guy quit on me for finding Jesus. My mama used to talk to me about Jesus all the time." And there we sat, having a full conversation about my new faith, and then we got up, shook hands, and I drove home.

When I got back, I asked Samantha again if we could sell. She had already said no several times, but this time she was just quiet, with no response at all. To me, that was a yes because it wasn't a no, and we began the journey of selling our businesses.

We started the process of selling, and it was a lot more complicated than I ever imagined. I know how to start stuff, but I don't know how to end it. I had no idea how to even go about it.

The people that worked for us in the company had been there for over ten years, and we were very close. Samantha's younger brother, Drew, had been working for us since the beginning, and we had invested so much in his life. He wasn't just a brother-in-law to me, he was a brother.

I had known Drew since he was fourteen years old, and I remember one day when he was dropped off at the warehouse for us to deal with, tweaking from drugs. I took him to meetings, and he looked up to me because I was so successful and made so much money. But I only knew how to give Drew what I had, and what I had to give him was all my character defects, which he soaked right up. I gave him a job at eighteen, and he grew up in the company with us. He became important and invaluable, and was our best buyer—even better than me. Our sellers would call and tell me how much he had talked them down. I told him, "You know, you have to let people make *some* money," and he just smiled. He was loyal to the core with a heart of gold, and he was really good at what he did. Eventually, he told me he wanted to sell, and I told him if he could get five accounts I would let him. He sat at lunch and cold called until he got five, and eventually became the second best salesman of the company.

Drew and Samantha were incredibly close, a bond that was part sister, part friend, and part mom. They were knit together in a special way, and having him around and in our lives was important and special for us both.

And it's how we felt about everyone who worked for us. Many of them I had hired out of twelve-step programs. They had been loyal and we were close friends. It wasn't just a business, it was a family.

This was, by far, the hardest part of letting go. But I'm not going to lie: the money was hard to let go of too. One of my companies was pulling in over a million dollars a year, and it was just free money; I didn't even have much to do with it. Another one of my video on demand Internet sites made $150,000 a month. But I just wanted out.

One afternoon I went to the Playboy headquarters to try and get an offer, and as I walked into the building, it was so swanky— fifteen stories high and filled with all the people I used to want to be. But as I looked around at it all, I just didn't want it anymore.

I sold the whole company for what I would have made in a year and a half. The accountant told me not to go about it the way I did. He told me that I was losing money, that the guy I was accepting an offer from was going to make payments, and I had no collateral, but I didn't care. Even if I didn't end up making my money back, I didn't want to haggle over it, I just wanted it done. I wanted out.

I sold Devil's Films on July 30, 2013, and when I showed up to sign the paperwork it was bigger than a telephone book; I didn't have a clue what I was signing, but I knew it was right. Twenty-six hours before, I sat down and inscribed these words in my journal:

> *I have 26 hours until I end the ownership of an empire that I built and a half a decade of a life that gave me worldly wealth while claiming countless victims. I am at peace with our decision to let go and let God. 33 years I ran from God and anyone or anything that resembled what I didn't want. But just over two years ago, a man sat in my car and prayed. That man said, "God knew what He got when He got you," and his acceptance of my under-world opened my heart to Christ. Now, after selling*

not one, but two multimillion dollar businesses, for
two years, I boldly lay down my life to serve and
am excited to see what His plans are for me.

Sometimes I still wrestle with whether or not I did the right thing. I know I needed to get out, but even though my profit was small, I know by selling it the work we started kept going. It was hard for me to resolve, and yet, I still had such a connection to the people who worked for me. I didn't want them to be out of a job; I wanted each of them to go on the same journey I had to get to the place where I was ready to walk away from it all. I didn't want to force it on them.

I am not an expert at what to do in the moments that I do them. I just kept trying to do what felt like the next right move. Some people have said that I should have burned it all to the ground and that I should go on a crusade against the adult entertainment industry—that I could be a frontrunner on a crusade and a kingpin for the kingdom. But I've been a kingpin all my life and that's just not what I'm about anymore.

What I'm about is being there to pull someone out of a life if they want to change. I hope that along the way some of the people who are still in the industry will see my life, see the hope I've found, and see that the courage to walk away and walk in the light is worth losing every single penny.

As soon as the sales of the companies were final, I got baptized by Jen's husband, T. D., and my lead pastor, Mike Hickerson. It was an amazing experience! I had finally turned the corner. I'd been on this journey for two years; I was saved, redeemed, a new creation, and ready to walk a whole new way! Coming up out of that water was as great as I expected, and I felt so free.

But do you know what's so amazing about grace? Grace is free. I didn't earn it, and there's nothing I could do to lose it. In that moment, I knew that was true like never before. But here's what else is amazing about grace. Grace is that God loves us right where we are, but way too much to leave us there. Grace? Grace is free. But growth? Growth takes participation.

So, by the grace of God, my story of redemption doesn't end here. This moment was actually just the beginning. My redemption story happens every single day, still to this day, but, I'm getting ahead of myself. What I still had to learn right after this moment was that even though I was saved, if I was going to grow into this new creation I had become, I still had a lot of participation up ahead before I was going to be free.

chapter eleven

WELCOME HOME

had always heard the pastor of my church say that there is nothing magic about the water you get baptized in, but sometimes, I wish there was. I wish it was that simple, like once you come out of that water, there's no more appetite for sin, no more arguing with your wife, and no more greed, lust, or envy—like dunk and done … BAM! Finished with all my character defects.

That's just not how it was. I found myself living as a new creation, but I still struggled to live a new way. Samantha and I went in and out of sobriety after we moved to Ventura. We knew we were addicts, but every once in a while we would drink and return to some old places in us where we felt safe and comfortable. Plus, we felt strong, and one of the worse things an addict can feel is self-sufficient.

Staying sober and clean just kept feeling harder and harder; I started finding myself saying I could just have one drink now and then, and every time I went out of town, I would drink a lot. So I went out of town a lot. Samantha and I took trips to New York, Hawaii, Tennessee. I would come back and tell the church and my pastor friends what I had done, as if they were a priest in confessional, and I hung my head low and tried to start over.

I didn't know why it kept happening. I couldn't understand it. I'd given it all over, I sold my businesses. I was serving God now, I was his agent, and I believed his love for me like never before. I also loved him back like never before, but I couldn't figure out how to make this area of my life change. What was wrong with me?

We had six months clean when we decided to go to Vegas. We kind of knew we shouldn't go, but it was my daughter's twenty-first birthday and that was still what we thought would best celebrate her in style. I remember Samantha and I told each other, "We won't drink." But, we did.

Vegas was like an old shoe. We had been going there two or three times a year to do the adult shows. We got married there, and there was even a time where we went for twelve years in a row and didn't have a single drink.

But, we didn't do anything small or anything cheap. We decided for the first night of this twenty-first birthday celebration it was going to be Vegas, "King Keith style." It was just like the good old days. We had a limo and VIP experiences everywhere we went. I was tossing out hundred-dollar bills, and we sang karaoke and laughed. My kids thought I was crazy. It seemed like we were having so much fun.

But the next morning wasn't so much fun. We had hangovers, and like any high, when you're coming down, you need another, and a little more than last time. I remembered a drug dealer I knew in town, so I looked him up to see if he would sell me some cocaine. We left our kids to go do their own thing, and I can't even really remember what happened until the next Monday morning.

We were leaving the next day, and I came down to the casino to try and find Samantha. I had been up all night and looked like it with white powder on my shirt. When I found her, she just looked at me, completely appalled.

"I don't know if this is going to work," she said. "You need to be a man and lead this family in the right direction, and right now, you disgust me."

Her words hit me hard, and I decided if I was so disgusting, I would just leave. I jumped in a taxi and went to another hotel. I complained to the driver about what my wife had just said, and it isn't funny, but it kind of makes me laugh now thinking about what he must have thought of me as he looked at my cracked lips and bloodshot eyes in his rearview mirror and listened to my version of the story. I looked back at him and said, "Well, what do you think?" He just said, "I think you should listen to your wife."

He dropped me off at a low-ranking hotel with my two suitcases in my hand, and I fumbled to the door, not knowing where I was going or what I was doing. I decided as soon as I walked in that I should go back and find Samantha.

I got back in the taxi and went back to the other hotel, and there she was, sitting at the same slot machine. We flew the kids home that night at midnight, and after they left, Samantha started having pain in her chest. She felt like she was going to have a heart attack. We hadn't done any drugs for several hours, but we were still drinking, taking "medicine" to come down off the high. She told me that she needed to go to the hospital, but we were both too exhausted and out of it to try and figure it out. Suddenly, I realized that she was really scared.

We jumped in a taxi, and I told her not to tell anybody that she did coke because they would arrest us. It felt like we were driving forever. I don't know why they have those hospitals so far away from the strip—seems like they should be right in the middle. When we got to the hospital, the first thing Samantha said was that she had been doing coke. They hooked her up to an IV drip and gave her some sedatives to calm her down, and we made it back to the hotel around 2 a.m.

I kept replaying Samantha's words in my head, "You disgust me," and I just kept thinking, *I disgust me.* At least we were finally on the same page about something.

We slept most of the day, when we finally made it back home, and the next morning I called my friend Jen. We were supposed to be working on this book together (the one that you're reading right now), but I knew I couldn't hide what had just happened.

"How was Vegas?" she asked, though I could tell she probably already knew. I must have looked horrible, and as I told her the story, I found myself confessing but almost joking through the words.

Jen sat across the table from me, and she wasn't laughing. Hearing that Samantha had gone to the hospital upset her. She and Samantha had become incredibly close friends, and I was treating it like it wasn't a big deal. Jen was torn up. I hadn't protected my wife. We were in a community now, and what we did didn't just affect us anymore, it affected everyone. Jen's eyes welled with tears.

I wanted to get on with talking about the book, and started bringing up something to talk about, but she just sat there quietly. She looked down at the table in the booth we had sat at so many times recording my story and played with some grains of salt on the table. Then she looked back at me and said, "Keith, I don't think you're ready to write this book; you just wrote a whole new chapter.

"You need help," she said. "You've been sober on and off for a long time, but you need to go to a twelve-step program and actually do the work, do the steps, and get well. Until you do that, I don't think we have a story to write yet. I care way too much about you to let you write this kind of book until you're ready to get well."

I'd like to tell you I listened. I'd like to tell you that I understood where she was coming from and heard her truth. I'd like to tell you that I humbled myself in that moment and admitted that I needed help. But, the truth is that my pride and ego were so hurt. I only pretended to listen and left so angry. How dare she tell me this! In that moment, I decided I was done. I was done with church, done with these people, and done with God. It clearly wasn't working for me, maybe I was just one of those people who couldn't get better.

I walked out of the restaurant steaming, and as soon as I left, my phone buzzed. It was my friend Dusty. I knew Dusty from the industry; we had been friends many years. He had moved to Ventura and was living in a warehouse, taking baths in a kiddie pool and cooking on a grill. Before I went to Vegas, he called me and asked if he could borrow money, but I knew he was using. I told him no and told him he needed to take a different path—you know, like me. I told him that I was going to take my daughters to Vegas, but as soon as I got back, I'd go with him to a meeting—for his sake.

The text said, "Hey, bro, we going to that meeting?" It was 10 a.m. on a Tuesday morning. I was still detoxing from the weekend and my conversation with Jen. I did *not* want to go to that meeting, but I knew what Samantha had said to me, and with Jen's words fresh in my mind, I texted back, "K." Maybe this would get everybody off my back.

I pulled up to pick him up and as soon as Dusty opened the door I said, "How many days you got? And be honest because I've got today."

He said, "Two days."

I went into that meeting and sat there with Dusty and couldn't quit coughing. (I don't know how people could figure out I had a problem or that I was a newcomer.) I sat there so beat up and broken and started to listen as people shared. It sounded like every one of them was telling my story. It was like they were all speaking directly to me. Then, when the meeting was over, there was this guy that I recognized from my neighborhood. I'd seen him around, and he'd come into the yogurt shop a few times, and I knew he had a lot of money, even more than me, but there was something different about him.

He was sitting in an iron chair in flip-flops, shorts, and a flat-bill hat. I knew he went to two meetings a day, and he drove a very unimpressive Toyota Tundra. He wasn't trying to impress anyone with his car or his watches or his money; he was just a regular guy. He came up to me after the meeting and said, "You need a sponsor?" I don't know why, but I said, "OK." He told me he'd meet me at the park, and we'd start reading through the steps of the program together.

So, we started meeting and reading. I'd read a paragraph, he read a paragraph, and we swapped. I thought it was amazing that this man would take the time out of his life to do that for me. I felt like I wasn't worth that hour.

We got to the first step, which was to admit that I was powerless. In the past, I might have admitted that I was powerless, but I never really bought it. He told me I had to have it in my gut, that I had to know I was powerless.

But something happened when I accepted that. I had lied to myself for so long that I could write a book of lies. I would see people having a beer on a sunny day on the beach, and I thought, *Why can't I have a beer on a sunny day on the beach? What's the harm in that?* But the thing is, when I drank that beer, I never made it to the beach; I wound up locked in my house alone, beating myself up like a bird plucking its feathers.

Everyone used to tell me when I went through the program that I only had to change one thing: *everything*. I had always refused to change everything; I thought if I let go of *everything*, then I would have *nothing* left. It was all the things I was holding onto that made me worth *something*. For the first time, this time, I got it down in my gut and said, "I am powerless. I give up 100 percent."

We talked about what to do with this powerlessness. He knew enough of my story with God, and he said that he felt like I had a good handle on who to give the power to. The next thing he asked me to do was not so easy. His instructions were to go home and write down everything I didn't want to tell him about myself from the time I was born until today. I was in this program for twelve years, and every time I got a sponsor, this was the last step and the last they heard from me.

I had stuff in my life that I was going to take to the grave with me, but I started to realize that refusing to go to the depths of those places and deal with them was ending me up right back here, where I didn't want to be. So this time, I just decided I didn't have anything to lose, and frankly, I didn't have anything else to do. I decided I didn't know if it was gonna work, but I was gonna try it and buy into this thing—go all in, and for some reason, I really trusted this man.

I sat down to write. And I wrote everything I could think of. Some of it I couldn't even put into sentences it was so painful to think about. When I was done with my list, I called him up.

We sat down and he said, "OK. Let's have it." And for the next three hours I sat there and told him everything I could think of— everything that I could never have imagined telling another soul. Everything that had piled on me for years and years—stuff from my childhood that had just piled on more and more shame and guilt and fear until I just began to stop feeling and ignored it and ran from it. Today, I was staring it down, confronting it head on.

And as I was confronting it, even more was getting exposed.

Among my list of shortcomings, I knew I had to list my addiction to pornography. Getting out of the porn industry didn't mean that I wasn't suffering from porn addiction, but this was the first time I had admitted it to anyone. It was the most humiliating thing to tell another man, but it was freeing too. Over the years, I had been so overexposed and become too accustomed to this part of my life. My sponsor challenged this thinking and encouraged me to find sobriety from pornography at the same time I found it from drugs and alcohol, and that day became another new sober date for me.

The next step was to take those things and give them to God. I had already given my life to Christ, but I had never given my stuff to him. I took that list and sat for an hour with it in front of me and humbly asked my Creator to remove those shortcomings and defects from me.

I had been saved for a long time. Now I felt free.

At the same time, Samantha had decided she was going to get well too, with or without me, and started going to a program on her own, found her own sponsor, and was working her own steps. We got to share our change together, but for the first time it wasn't dependent on the other. We were both doing the hard work of getting well.

Things were starting to change within me. I felt a connection with God like never before, and now it was time to make things right with people. I went back as far as I could, and I made a list of many of the people I had hurt and, though I'm sure it could have been longer, it had around twenty-eight people on it who I knew I needed to find.

One of the people on that list was Guy. He lived eight houses down from us and used to play basketball with me and the other neighborhood kids on the goal Grandmugie had constructed by digging a hole, putting a pole in the ground, and pouring concrete around it. We wore the grass down in her driveway and yard playing H-O-R-S-E.

During those years when I was hanging out with Donnie, we tried to figure out ways to get more money and drugs. One afternoon we walked by Guy's house and the front door was open. We went in and stole his bass guitar and his mom's jewelry. We pawned it and bought drugs. We did it, and I never looked back.

During my amends process, I actually found Guy on Facebook, and I knew he was one of those boulders I had to put on my list; I had to see this guy. I googled his name and a phone number came up. I called it, and his mom answered the phone. I told her I was looking for Guy, and she just said, "Who is this?" I ended up winning her over enough for her to give me his number. I called him and told him I was coming to Memphis and would like to meet up.

I guess I needed to plan a trip to Memphis. It had taken me years to get to this willingness.

I checked into a hotel, and I had my list. Some were living, and some were not. I visited my mother and Grandmugie's graves. They were buried together in Flat Rock, Mississippi, and I made my amends to them there. There was another grave I knew I had to visit, though I wasn't even sure where to go. I called my aunt, my mom's surviving sister, and asked her if she knew where my half-brother Dathan had been buried. She didn't know; no one knew. They just knew he had been buried in Mississippi, but I knew I had to find it.

I researched and found an old picture on the Internet with a little slate piece of concrete that has his name on it. It said Horn Lake, Mississippi, so I drove there with my father. We stopped in this little town and asked where the cemetery was. When we arrived, no one was there, no workers, no plot directory, nothing—just land with grey tombstones on it. We started walking and looking, reading names and looking at every grave. I was almost ready to give up when my dad hollered, "Keith, I found it!"

That was the first time I was able to find closure and grieve all that had happened. I stood there and thought about all that we had been through and all the ways I had hurt and failed him, and I wept there at his grave and made my amends.

That first day in Memphis was a reflection of giving honor to the people that I had hurt who I could no longer sit face-to-face with. I knew it was obviously more for me than them, but it was an important step for me to make things right.

I drove by both of my grandparents' houses, occupied by new families now, and memories came flooding back—all of them—the good, the bad, the painful, and the grateful. It was overwhelming.

The next day I made amends to my sisters and went to find my Pentecostal stepfather. I arrived in his shop, and I sat with him for three hours. He still carried that little New Testament Bible in his back pocket and told everyone who walked through the door about Jesus. From the moment I saw him, it was in a new light. I saw that he wasn't prejudiced against anyone; he immediately loved all of them, and he looked different to me.

I explained to him why I was there. He looked back too and said, "You were just a kid back then, and I wasn't a great guy either." I was beginning to see why this step mattered—how important it was to my healing and all those memories—the things I had done, the things he had done—all of it was beginning to heal and started to feel like grace.

When I finally got to Guy, I met him in a coffee shop. When we sat down, he was puzzled and didn't know why we were meeting after so many years. I told him I was there to sweep my side of the street, but I didn't expect the moment to go the way it did. I was flooded with emotion, and tears began to roll down my cheeks. I felt a deep sense of how he must have felt. I asked him for forgiveness. I reached in my pocket and handed him the money that I felt those items would have been worth.

We sat and continued talking, and he told me that he had become a pastor. How on earth did I ever get to a place in my life to know so many pastors? He added me to his weekly email he sends out, and to this day it's one of my favorite things to pop up in my inbox.

During my stay in Memphis, I had ninety days sober from alcohol, but my sobriety from my porn addiction was much more fresh. When I got to the hotel room at the end of that emotionally exhausting day, I was ready to escape. I turned on the TV, and there it came across the screen, "Adult Viewing." Then I did something that was very atypical for me at the time. I called a guy who had become my prayer partner. His name was David, and I had met him one Sunday at church.

I picked up the phone, and he met me with such grace and simply said, "Well, let's just pray." We got on our knees, and even though I was in that hotel room and he was in Kentucky, we prayed.

As we did, I felt strength come over me, and it got me through the night. All it took was calling my spiritual sponsor, telling on myself and talking about it. Once again, bringing things to the light did away with the darkness.

We finished up in Mississippi, and I came home and made amends with my ex-wife and my two daughters. I knew that I had another daughter out there somewhere. I had heard that Cindy had a baby girl who I had abandoned long ago, and sometimes these types of amends do more harm than good, but my sponsor told me that I should find her. I found out that she was living in

Bakersfield. I went and sat with her over breakfast and asked to make amends for any harm or suffering I had caused her. The conversation went well, and we sat and talked for a long time. A couple months later, I was able to return and meet her five children, my grandchildren, and speak to two hundred men at her church and tell them my story. Samantha got to meet them too.

One of the most powerful amends I made was with Samantha. We were coming up on our eighteenth year of marriage, and there was so much I could cover. But, even though we worked in the pornography industry together for over ten years, one of the most important amends I had to make was for watching pornography throughout our marriage. At first, her response was that she had excused it, thinking that's what all men did, but once we dug deeper, we realized how much it had had hurt her and how much it had come between us, robbing us of true intimacy and closeness. She met me with such grace and tenderness and forgave me.

Once I finished my list, I thought I had done all my amends, but suddenly it occurred to me that I had one more. There was one person on that list who I had never made amends to: God. I found some quiet space and went to him and apologized to my Father for the pain and suffering I had caused him all those years that I had been running from him. I asked him to forgive me for all the times I had turned against him or blamed him or cursed his name. It's funny that I thought of him last because now I try and think of him first. I could not imagine a better way to wrap up that process: to meet him after I had done my best to make it right with everyone else and hear him speak to me once again and say, *Welcome home.*

chapter twelve

TAKE UP YOUR MAT
AND WALK

I remember when Drew, my brother-in-law, completed the twelve steps, a friend of mine asked him, "Well, what now?" And he said something so profound, "Well, I guess I start back at number one." And I'm not going to lie, it kind of made me mad. But if you look closely at the last few steps of the program, he was exactly right. The point of this journey is not to get finished and arrive and be done. The point of the journey is the journey. And now, my job is to go back through the steps, but this time take someone else who needs them with me.

It's funny to me to think about how long I had been in the program—eighteen years—and how *no one* ever asked me for anything. I was never asked to speak at a meeting, never asked to be anyone's sponsor, never asked to help anybody. The thing is that you can't give away something you don't have.

I guess that's maybe why Jesus says when you try and keep your life, you'll lose it, but when you lose your life for his sake, you'll actually find it (Matthew 16:25). Real life is found when we give ours away.

And I've found this to be true. Since I have lived in the final steps of my program and shifted my perspective from how to hang on to how I can give it away, everything has changed for me. When I keep all my new growth to myself, it just dies, but if I replant it in others, it keeps growing something new in me. I've had a good amount of money for a long time, but I have never been this rich.

And that deep richness in me made me stop feeling the need to prove to people that I was somebody. I stopped trying to use people and just started to help them. The things I needed around me to make me feel like I was somebody, just didn't matter to me anymore. The thirty thousand dollar watches I owned, I just couldn't wear them; they felt weird on my wrist because they just didn't match who I was anymore.

And, if you can believe it, I even sold my S65, and, while I would be lying to you if I said sometimes I didn't miss it, I just knew that I couldn't have it anymore. I used to lead with the watch, lead with the car, lead with the money, but now I didn't need it. I was leading with a new way of life.

But this new life has afforded me all the things that matter most. I'll never forget going to Jaxon's school on career day. I showed up with cups of yogurt for each kid, which basically gave me hero status. I watched them pass them around the room, and I was struck by how big the moment was. Here I was being the dad I always dreamed of having. My firefighting dad never showed. When my girls were young, I couldn't tell their school about my career, but now, because of how God had rescued me, I could have this moment with my son.

"You've only got to change one thing," they said, "*everything*."

They were right, but changing everything has meant everything to me. I thought it would leave me empty; rather, it has made me whole. I thought it would leave me lonely; it has given me community. I thought it would kill me, but it has given me life.

Life is no longer about me, thank goodness, because I'm just not that interesting.

I used to have a handicap placard hanging on my car that I had gotten somewhat illegally, which I often used to whip into a spot up close, stealing it from someone who actually needed it. I remember the day I got rid of that thing once and for all. I had met my friend Mike Breaux for breakfast, and, without even thinking about it, pulled into the disabled parking spot right in front of the restaurant. When I opened the door, Mike walked over to my car, pointed to the handicap sticker and said, "Give me that!" I said, "Why?" He stated the obvious, "Because you aren't disabled!" I reached up and took it down and handed it to him and said, "Yeah, I guess God healed me."

He gave it back to me a week later, and it was nailed to a cross that he had made from some pallet wood. Underneath it said, "Take up your mat and walk." I still keep it hanging in my garage to this day.

And that's what I'm trying to do with my life. How do I change everything? One day at a time. Minute by minute, piece by piece, and one thing at a time.

Sometimes people talk about how God has a big old eraser, and he just erases your past, but I think he does one better. I think, since he's a carpenter, he actually takes all those broken pieces and makes something new. He takes your past and then uses it to create something better, something usable, actually. In fact, I don't just think that. I know it because that is what he has done with me.

Today, I can't even imagine the man I used to be. I don't even really like to talk about that man, and that's why I wrote a book. So I could just hand it to people when they asked about my life and just say, "Here, read this." But the truth is that this story is not my story. It's God's story, and the whole point of it is that I don't want you to miss out on the fact that he is also writing one in you.

Part Two

The Tools

The journey of writing this book has been an incredible one, and, as you have seen, even the writing of it has been a transformational one. But I didn't just want to write my story to tell my story; I wanted to help people. So, after finishing the journey, my friend and mentor Mike Breaux and I started talking about the tools that got me here, and he agreed to help me put this second half into words.

We have taken the steps of the program that has helped me so much and put them into the acronym *BREATHE*:

B: *Admit My **B**rokenness*
R: ***R**elinquish Control*
E: ***E**valuate My Life with Fearless Honesty*
A: *Make **A**mends*
TH: ***TH**ink a Whole New Way*
E: ***E**ncourage Others with My Life and Story*

And these aren't just steps for recovery from addictions. This is the way we were all meant to live. I hope they encourage and help you as much as they have me, and most importantly, I pray they will get you to a place where you can *Just Breathe.*

chapter thirteen

ADMIT
MY BROKENNESS

have learned the hard way that there is a big difference between being broken and being miserable. As you can probably tell from the pages before this one, I have been miserable *a lot*. Being miserable is being uncomfortable; it's hating circumstances; it's being self-absorbed; and it's getting caught. Brokenness? That comes from a different place, and it's the first step to finding the pathway to freedom because it's brokenness that gets you to the place where you're finally willing to admit that there is something broken in you—something that you can't fix. There's a deep realization when you figure out that your way is not the right way. That's when you're finally ready to cooperate and get well.

I've always thought the self-help section of a bookstore was a funny category. It seems like kind of an oxymoron to me. I mean, if self could help self, why would you need a book on how to help yourself? And when you're truly broken, that becomes the biggest realization: you can't help you anymore.

When I started to become familiar with the Bible I really loved reading about Jesus and all of his encounters with people—people like me.

In John, chapter 5, Jesus' heart is filled with compassion for a guy who he miraculously heals. The man was broken and had been an invalid for thirty-eight years. It's an amazing story of new beginnings, but this story contains what I've come to know as one of the most important questions for life and recovery. It's one of the most important questions to ask if you want to tell the difference between whether you are truly broken or just miserable. Before Jesus even touched the man, Jesus asked him, "Do you want to get well?" (John 5:6 NIV).

When I first read that story, I thought that was a stupid question. But after years of my own stubborn refusal to change and working with all kinds of people who are living in denial, I've discovered that's not a stupid question. It's actually one of the most important questions we can ask ourselves. Sure, we are miserable, sick, know we have a problem, know things are out of control, but do we *really* want to get well?

Maybe it's fear that keeps us from getting well and walking free. Maybe we've created an image for ourselves that we feel like we have to keep, and we put on a mask and pretend we're fine. Or maybe it's fear of discovery and the subsequent fear of rejection. We think, *If they know the real me, then no one will like me, accept me, or want to be around me.* And that fear keeps us paralyzed, keeps us saying, *There's no way I can show weakness, and reaching out is a sign of weakness. Besides, I've got this; I can handle this; and I can beat this thing on my own.*

Isn't it crazy how we can fear *change* more than we fear the damage the addiction or the hurt is doing to us? As miserable as we are, we would rather wear that habit like a comfortable pair of old shoes than go through the challenge of breaking in a new pair and walking a much better, new direction.

I can't remember the moment that I finally decided that I did want to get well. I think it was somewhere between my chapped-lipped-white-powder-on-my-shirt-cocaine-bender trip to Vegas and that three-block drive to tell my sponsor everything I had ever done. And somewhere in there, by the grace of God, I was able to drop the fear and finally humble myself to the loving touch of Jesus, and he started healing me. I also got into a community of fellow strugglers, where I encountered honest, loving people and a loving God who met me where I was. Still, I never would have made it to that place without finally admitting that, on my own, I am a broken, shattered mess.

So, I know that no matter what you struggle with, if you will humbly allow God to go to work on the inside of you, if you will cooperate with him by working some steps, and if you will link arms with honest, fellow-strugglers, you will begin to get a handle on and actually overcome and break the chains of what binds you up and walk free.

So, what is it that keeps you from walking free? What do you struggle with?

Anxiety? Worry? Panic? Anger? Bitterness? Abuse? Is it gambling? Alcohol? Meth? Heroine? Painkillers? Pornography? Sexual addiction? Maybe bigotry? Cynicism? Lying? Criticism? Are you a control freak? Workaholic? Perfectionist? Procrastinator? Do you overspend? Overeat? Not eat enough? Do you have relational wounds that have left you with some trust issues? Made you codependent? Do you ever know something is wrong, but you do it anyway? Do you ever want to change your language but still spew out profanity? Do you often find it hard to go to sleep? Do you often find it hard to get out of bed? Do you struggle with depression? Do you battle with envy, discontentment, or insecurity? Got a memory that haunts you? Got some unresolved guilt that paralyzes you?

If you answered yes to any of those questions, then welcome to the human race! We *all* need to "get well" in some way. We are *all* in recovery from something. So this is for *everybody*, unless you're perfect, which you aren't. None of us are.

We say this definition of insanity a lot in twelve-step meetings: "Insanity is doing the same things over and over, expecting different results." Sometimes when I was writing my story I would get exhausted with it because reliving all those things and moments when I was making the same mistake over and over again just wore me out! Maybe you even felt like that when you were reading it!

Paul wrote these words about himself, "I don't understand myself at all, for I really want to do what is right, but I can't. I do what I don't want to—what I hate. I know perfectly well that what I am doing is wrong ... but I can't help myself because I'm no longer doing it. It is sin inside me that is stronger than I am that makes me do these evil things" (Romans 7:15–17 TLB).

Ever felt like that?

Now, if you are a Jesus follower, those cycles of mistakes don't define who you are. Paul is not beating himself up here. In fact, he has just written in previous verses about how he's been rescued by Jesus' grace and power. He knows that his true identity is that of a much-loved child of God.

But, at the same time, he is honestly acknowledging the very real struggle that goes on within each of us. The struggle that all the image management, all the willpower, all the prideful self-help, and all the playing God is not going to fix.

I know what he's talking about. I've been there. You probably have too. You give in to that addiction or that habit and then you crash in a pile of guilt and make futile promises to yourself, that you're never going to do this again. I've never been very good at math, but I've finally learned the power of this equation: Self-deception + Self-reliance = Self-destruction.

That math works every time, but I'm learning that freedom starts to come when you stop kidding yourself and stop looking to your own strength to fix yourself.

Unfortunately, it is human nature that, most of the time, we won't change until the pain becomes greater than the fear of change. We don't change until the marriage starts to disintegrate, until we get the phone call in the middle of the night, or until we wake up on someone's bathroom floor, in an emergency room, or in a jail cell.

A friend of mine once said, "Healing didn't happen to me until the acid of my pain finally ate through the wall of my denial." And, I suppose that's one way to go, but I wonder if we could save ourselves some pain, see the light today, and start swimming toward the surface. Some say that you have to hit "rock bottom," but I say, actually, you don't.

Well, with regard to humility, you actually do. You do have to be broken and sincerely want to get well. But, you don't have to hit rock bottom. Like a buddy of mine says, "You don't have to ride the elevator all the way down … you can jump off on the third floor." You don't have to hurt yourself and a whole lot of other people who love you anymore. So, whether you've hit rock bottom, or you think you might have a couple more falls in you, why not just get off the elevator now? Why not see the light, drop the denial, humble yourself, and answer Jesus' question today with a, "Yes! I want to get well!"

I'm also learning the truth of this verse: "We felt we were

doomed to die and saw how powerless we were to help ourselves; but that was good, for then we put everything into the hands of God, who alone could save us, for he can even raise the dead" (2 Corinthians 1:9 TLB).

There's power in powerlessness! When we drop the denial, humble ourselves, and admit our weakness, then God's strength has permission to begin to flow through us and helps us break these cycles in our life. And the most amazing part about God is that he does it with love.

Check out these words directly from the mouth of the living God: "'I have seen what they do, but I will heal them anyway! I will lead them. I will comfort those who mourn, bringing words of praise to their lips. May they have abundant peace, both near and far,' says the LORD, who heals them" (Isaiah 57:18–19).

Did you hear what God says? He says he knows all about what you are doing. You don't embarrass him. You don't disgust him. He really wants to heal you! If you are feeling lost, he wants to lead you. If you're feeling overwhelmed, he wants to comfort you. If you're worried, anxious, stressed out, confused, and scared, he wants to give you peace. If you feel like you're drowning, he wants to rescue you. He will help you break through the surface and breathe!

Bill W., one of the founders of Alcoholics Anonymous, referring to his and others' miraculous relief from alcoholism, once wrote, "We found that God could and would if he were sought."*

Our loving Father gives us a choice through the double-edged sword of free will. He asks, *Do you want to get well?* because the surrender of our will to the will and supernatural power of God is the pathway to freedom.

---

* W. and Smith, *Alcoholics Anonymous*, 60.

The power lies in the admission of powerlessness.

The first words to come out of Jesus' mouth as he launched into his famous sermon on the mount were, "Blessed are the broken." Blessed are those who know that they are busted. How fortunate are those who will acknowledge their spiritual bankruptcy, humble themselves, and hunger for God. They will find that God *could and would,* if only he were sought. If this is true, then it is also possible that God can't and won't if he is *not.* What would it take for you today to get off the downward spiral right here and admit that you need a Savior. Maybe it's time to ask yourself that question, *Do you want to get well?* Friend, there is no better day to surrender than today.

chapter fourteen

RELINQUISH CONTROL

What comes to your mind when you think of the word *surrender*? I used to always have negative images in my mind when I thought of that word, like it was kind of bad news. Like somebody getting slammed up against a police car or a guy with his head covered in front of a firing squad.

But I'm learning that the true definition of surrender is to give control to someone else. I like that definition, even though it doesn't really look like what I've always thought. It describes that there is a choice of the person surrendering to "give up control." True surrender isn't a forced act. It's not mindless but a choice to let go and give the use of something to someone else, someone who is stronger, more capable, and more powerful than me.

And it's actually good news. Getting to a place of true brokenness—not just being miserable but being broken—gets us to a place where we are ready to take the next step: *surrender*.

Can I tell you why it took me so long to surrender? There was this thing in me that kept me relying on my own power. There was this thing in me that kept me from seeking help. In fact, this thing is in you too.

It's what keeps us running and competing in some unhealthy ways. This thing causes us to lie about our pasts. It makes us exaggerate our accomplishments, enhance our social media profile, lie about our weight, and pad our résumés. It keeps us from learning new things. It forces us to cheat instead of lose. It won't let us celebrate when other people win. It even makes us feel good when someone else fails. It makes us buy stuff to impress people. This thing stands in the way of not only our relationships with other people but also our relationship with God, and ironically, it does a number on us too.

You may have guessed it by now, but you know what this thing is? It's pride.

I appreciate the way Beth Moore writes about it in this poem:

> My name is Pride. I am a cheater.
>
> I cheat you of your God-given destiny … because you demand your own way.
>
> I cheat you of contentment … because you "deserve better than this."
>
> I cheat you of knowledge … because you already know it all.
>
> I cheat you of healing … because you are too full of me to forgive.
>
> I cheat you of holiness … because you refuse to admit when you are wrong.
>
> I cheat you of vision … because you'd rather look in the mirror than out the window.

I cheat you of genuine friendship … because nobody's ever going to know the real you.

I cheat you of greatness in heaven … because you refuse to wash another's feet on earth.

I cheat you of God's glory … because I convinced you to seek your own.

My name is Pride. I am a cheater.

You like me because you think I'm always looking out for you.

Untrue. I'm looking to make a fool out of you.

God has so much for you, I admit, but don't worry,

If you stick with me, you'll never know.*

We talk a lot about pride, self-centeredness, and ego in the twelve-step program because it's the real root of our addiction. We remind one another of what EGO stands for: Edging God Out. We can get so full of ourselves that there's no room for God. We start thinking, *I really* am *the center of the universe.* I think it's why the Bible says that God detests pride; it keeps us from experiencing his love, his acceptance, his power, and his leadership, which he knows could change everything.

My friend Mike Breaux showed me this verse I love; in fact, he has it tattooed on his calf. He says that when people ask him about it, he says, "Oh, it's a little three-step program I'm in." It says, "And what does the LORD require of you? To act justly and to love mercy and to walk humbly with your God" (Micah 6:8 NIV).

---

* Beth Moore, *Praying God's Word* (Nashville, TN: Broadman & Holman Publishers, 2000), 59–60.

Act justly. Love mercy. Walk humbly with God.

I'm finally learning that walking humbly with God is the best way to live. A wise man named Solomon, wrote, "Pride comes before being destroyed and a proud spirit comes before a fall" (Proverbs 16:18 NLV). You see, pride is a cheater. Humility is the key to recovery; we have to quit playing God and choose to surrender to his care and control.

Surrender begins with a willingness to believe that there is a God who is stronger than you. A God who is more powerful than you. A God who has the ability to rescue you and give you the power to live again. I'm learning that this simple willingness to believe changes the focus of your life. It begins to free you from the ever-tightening cycle of self-absorption and points you to help beyond your own inadequate strength.

But maybe that's a hurdle for you—even believing that there is a God. I can relate to that. I used to think that you had to believe in God in order to have faith in God, but I'm learning it's actually the other way around. Faith is putting hope in something you cannot see, so if you already believed you wouldn't actually need faith. You have to have faith so that you can believe.

And it doesn't take a gigantic faith. Not perfect faith. Not even unwavering faith. It just takes a little bit—just an earnest and sincere willingness to believe that there is a God who is more capable than you. He is capable of getting your life back on track.

When Jesus approached broken people, he simply wanted to know if there was a willingness to believe. I love one story where a man is looking for Jesus to heal his son. When Jesus asks if he believes, the man says, "I do believe; help me overcome my unbelief!" (Mark 9:24 NIV). I can relate to that.

Or maybe, for you, the hurdle is not so much believing in God but believing in a God who would actually care anything about you—believing in a God who would actually love you or have the power to help you. But maybe you've been believing in the wrong God.

That's what happened to me. I kept meeting the wrong God. Early on in my childhood I started believing that God was waiting around the corner to catch me doing something bad. I believed in a God who was strict and critical and only around on Sundays. A God who required unreasonable things from me and gave nothing in return. A God who would be like everyone else and alienate me because of who I was and what I did for a living.

I have a friend who has been sober for a long time now and has sponsored and helped all kinds of people. He would talk about how he met new guys in the recovery program and they said, "There's no way I would turn my life over to God! He'd ruin it and I'd probably deserve it."

He then helped them unpack their perception of their love-less, demanding, judgmental God. My friend told them, "You know what? You ought to fire that God of yours. You've got the wrong God for recovery. The God who operates here is loving, kind, encouraging, forgiving, honest, and will always be there for you. I had a God like yours when I first came in here, but I had to fire him and get a new God."

Now don't misunderstand me, there is only one God. It's just that the God many of us have learned to believe in is not the true and living God, and we need to fire our misperceptions of him.

I had to learn about the true character of a God who is love. That's why studying the life of Jesus has helped me so much. I believe that Jesus not only came to lay down his life for our sin but to show us what God is really like as well. He embraces outcasts, fights for the underdog, touches the untouchables, and mends the broken. It was eye-opening for me reading about Jesus and the way he interacted with people like me.

I love the way my friend Jodi Hickerson puts it in this spoken word:

> I have wanted to be in.
> To be in the "in" crowd,
> In the loop, in the know, among the proud,
> Not left out, but to be allowed
> To be in.
> I have wanted to be in.
>
> Wear clothes that are "in" style
> A trendsetter and versatile,
> Just the right cut, and a perfect smile,
> I have wanted to be in.
>
> To be looked at as someone who has much,
> All the "in" music on my iPod touch,
> Own the latest and greatest stuff and such,
> I have wanted to be in.
>
> But, I have felt aggravated,
> Frustrated,
> Unappreciated.
> Slated,
> As someone who is underrated,
>
> Unimportant, unknown, unseen,
> Average, mediocre, routine,
> Beneath, below, beyond a chance,
> Inconsequential, insignificant.

But Jesus, He met people like me,
Took notice of a blind man and made him see,
Saw a locked up kid, and set him free.
Told little Zacchaeus to get out of the tree,

Felt it when a desperate woman touched His cloak,
Kneeled beside a dead girl and up she woke,
Hung out with the down and out and broke,
Offered hope to the forgotten with just the words
    He spoke.

Touched a man with leprosy who others would mock,
Touched the mouths of the mute and at once they
    could talk,
Forgave a woman at a well, who was the laughing
    stock,
Came to be The Shepherd of a wandering flock.

In the company of sinners is where He would eat,
Defended an adulterer and made her accusers retreat,
Made followers out of men who were crooked cheats,
Let the tears of a prostitute anoint His feet,

And suddenly,
Dramatically,
Miraculously,
Undeniably
They were in.

In His story,
In His truth,
In His grace,
In His purpose,
In His eyes someone great,

And I have wanted to be in.

And since the day I met with Him,
He took all that I had been,
All my fear, my shame, my sin,
And changed my life by letting me in.

This God that we are surrendering to? He is a good God, a kind God, and a God who doesn't just put up with me but loves me—the kind of God who lets me *in*. Check out some of these Scriptures that helped me fire my "old God":

You keep track of all my sorrows. You have collected all my tears in your bottle. You have recorded each one in your book. (Psalm 56:8)

The LORD is like a father to his children, tender and compassionate to those who fear him. For he knows how weak we are; he remembers we are only dust. (Psalm 103:13–14)

Unfailing love surrounds those who trust the LORD. (Psalm 32:10)

Hope in the LORD; for with the LORD there is unfailing love. His redemption overflows. (Psalm 130:7).

"When you go through deep waters, I will be with you. When you go through rivers of difficulty, you will not drown. When you walk through the fire of oppression, you will not be burned up; the flames will not consume you." (Isaiah 43:2)

I need a God like that. You need a God like that. You need someone stronger than yourself.

Keith Miller, a Christian writer who went through a twelve-step recovery program in his own life, writes this in his book *Hunger for Healing*:

> As I watched the Higher Power reveal itself to various people in the group, it's personality always had certain definite familiar characteristics. I knew that if everyone were "making up" their own higher power, this wouldn't happen. It couldn't. The personality of the Higher Power revealed in those meetings was always loving and forgiving; gave people however many new starts needed to get into recovery and get well; was honest, moral, courageous, and strong, but never abusive; and was loyal beyond belief whether people deserved it or not. In fact, as I looked carefully at the Higher Power in the 12-step program, I realized that it had a haunting family resemblance to Jesus Christ.*

It's no accident or coincidence. He is Jesus Christ. And if you are entirely ready to surrender your life and your will to his loving care and control, then your sin, which is the really huge deal, will be forgiven, and you will start the process of becoming a new person who can walk free in the power and unfailing love of God.

I'm learning that the greatness of a man or woman is determined by the measure of their surrender. When you surrender, God moves in, and you will finally have the right person in charge of life and the right kind of power it takes to change. King Keith had to come down off the throne of his life and give God the control. I had to quit Edging God Out, had to drop my pride, and ask Jesus Christ to forgive my sin and lead my life.

And man, how he has changed my life! So much so, that it is

* Keith Miller, *Hunger for Healing* (New York: Harper Collins, 1946), n.p.

my greatest joy to keep surrendering my life to him every single day because he is a God who loves me. Every night before I go to bed, I put my phone in my house shoe, and tuck it under my bed. What I've found is that this forces me to get on my knees every morning to pick it up and every night to put it back, and while I'm down there, it has been pretty convenient to take that posture on my knees pretty intentionally and say morning and night, "My life is yours, Lord, I surrender. Do with me what you please." As a result, I'm beginning to walk free, and if you'll choose to surrender, you can do the same.

---

chapter fifteen

EVALUATE MY LIFE WITH FEARLESS HONESTY

What's the best gift you ever received as a kid for Christmas? A Play Station? An X-box? A Cabbage Patch Kid? A bike? A puppy? I remember one Christmas receiving that game called "Operation." Remember that game? You get to play surgeon on this cartoon guy that is laid out on the board. You have to carefully remove various "organs" without touching the sensitive sides surrounding them. If you accidentally make a mistake, it makes a horrible buzzing noise that shocks you, and his electronic red nose lights up, and it's "game over."

I certainly don't intend to light up anyone's nose in this chapter, and hopefully you won't get any kind of buzzing shock, but I do want to talk about the value of doing a little probing, a little dissecting, and a little "self-exploratory" surgery.

When I say "self-exploratory" don't mistake that for thinking you have to do this by yourself. I think we settled that in the last chapter. Self-help is an oxymoron. If self could help, then we wouldn't need "self-help." Self-help is kind of like decaf coffee. It looks like coffee, smells like coffee, tastes like coffee, but it lacks any real punch.

We're learning to be broken and surrendered people, so we know we need a power that self-help can't give. I need strength beyond my feeble willpower, and so do you. All of us need the supernatural help that is available to anyone who will admit their powerlessness and surrender their life and their will to God's care and control.

When we surrender our life and will to the care and control of Jesus Christ, he moves in and begins working from the inside out. I like how the Bible explains it. It says, "For God is working in you, giving you the desire and the power to do what pleases him" (Philippians 2:13). He is working in me giving me both the "want to" (desire) and the "how to" (power), to do what pleases him. That's pretty cool!

The good news is that you don't have to do this alone anymore. You weren't made to do it alone. None of us were; we were all made to do life with God. And when we walk away from our self-centeredness, our self-importance, and our self-reliance; when we stop trying to control everything, fix everything, and run everything; and when we begin to see ourselves with appropriate smallness and the God of the universe with appropriate hugeness, and realize he loves us anyway, it makes us more willing to ask for help.

And as we come to this self-exploratory surgery step, we need to remember that, in fact, it involves you, God, and eventually a trusted friend. There are different ways that various recovery programs talk about this, but I'm learning that, somewhere in the early stages of breaking free, you have to examine yourself with fearless honesty.

In my twelve-step program we call it taking a "fearless moral inventory." This is a huge inside out step. This has to do with coming clean, getting honest about the past, getting honest with the struggle, getting honest with God, taking off the mask, and telling ourselves and someone else the truth.

Every retailer and every business knows the importance of inventory. You have to ask, "What's in the store? What's in the warehouse? How much is in the bank? How's our stock doing? How's employee morale? What's really true about our situation right now?" Businesses that don't do that? Well, they don't usually last very long.

And people who won't do this step? Well, their recovery doesn't usually last very long either. This is a journey to the center of the truth, and this is the step that God wants every single one of us to take.

I'm kind of a new football fan. I didn't grow up playing sports, but my son is a little athletic guy so I'm learning so that I can hang with him. I've seen those NFL referees go to the replay monitor and take a closer look at the previous play. They'll come back onto the field and announce, "After further review, the call on the field is confirmed."

And it makes me think of how important it is for us to do that with God. It's always a good idea to come to God and say, "Search me, O God. Let's go to the replay monitor, rewind, and take a closer look at my character. I'd love to get your eyes on me, because you always make the right call. After further review, what do you see I need to work on?"

I think one of the deepest longings of the human heart is to be known and loved just the way we are. We long to know that somebody in this world knows everything about us and loves us anyway. I think there's something in us that thinks a love like that might be the very thing that changes us.

Author Richard Rohr writes, "Because God loves us uncon-ditionally—along with our dark sides—we don't need to dodge ourselves. In the light of this love the pain of self-knowledge can be at the same time the beginning of our healing."*

Remember that God says, "I have seen what they do, but I will heal them anyway!"

So, as you get ready to take this step, hear God say over you, *Don't be afraid. I already know what you've done. I already know what we will find as we take this journey together. Relax, I already know all your character defects. I have seen everything, but I want to heal you anyway!*

God is for you as you do this process. His steady gaze of unfailing love will guide you as you do this. And what do you have to lose? A bunch of garbage that needs to go to the curb? It's worth it.

To begin this self-exploratory surgery, I suggest you get alone and grab a scalpel—just kidding. It might be better to grab a pen and a spiral notebook or a laptop and sit down and say, "Search me, O God, and know my heart; test me and know my anxious thoughts. Point out anything in me that offends you, and lead me along the path of everlasting life" (Psalm 139:23–24).

Ask God to help you out. *What's the honest truth about me? What's wrong in me? What do I feel guilty about and why? What kind of resentment and bitterness do I have rolling around in there? Point out the things I've done, no matter how painful it might be to see them. What are some character defects in me that need chang-ing? God, I'm asking you to reveal me from the inside out.*

And he will. Better than any replay machine, any CAT scan, or MRI, and you can expect him to bring to mind some things

---

* Richard Rohr, *The Enneagram: A Christian Perspective* (New York: Crossroad Publishing, 2001), n.p.

that you didn't expect to come up. But that's what you want. It's about coming clean.

You can also expect something else to happen.

Just as the two of you are discovering the truth about you, a cold front will start moving in and that old dark cloud called denial will try to blanket you and blind you to the things you need to expose to the light.

And you'll find yourself saying, *Well, I guess that's really not that big of a deal. I'm not really like that. I don't need to write that down. I'm not letting go of that.* You'll mark through it, get the eraser going, or hit delete.

Now, you can see why the word *fearless* is used. Because to go deep within yourself and be ruthlessly honest is not an easy deal. To get beyond denial is a constant battle and seeing the naked truth is not exactly a trip to the local Dairy Queen, or, you know, Surf 'n Yogurt.

But here's the truth I've learned, "People who conceal their sins will not prosper, but if they confess and turn from them, they will receive mercy" (Proverbs 28:13). I've learned that the sin you want to *conceal* the most is the sin you need to *reveal* the most. And if the goal is getting well and walking free, then what's the point of hiding stuff?

Here's what you need to do next: get in a quiet, uninterruptible place where you can be still and think. Don't rush this. If this is a new experience for you, you'll need to set aside a large block of time. Pray the "Search me, O God" type prayer and start writing it down as God leads you.

Why write it down? It forces you to be more specific and focused. I've found that if I've thought about it, and I can say it and can write it down, then I've got a much clearer picture. If I can't, it's still pretty fuzzy. Sometimes I'll make a sweeping generalization, *God, I've really blown it.* And he responds, *Yes ... and?* Now, he certainly doesn't need the specifics, but we do. You have to face reality. It helps you stop denying problems and take responsibility for what you need to own.

I also like to write because, like a coach who can go back and review old game films to see how his team is improving, I can go back weeks or months and see how God has been moving in my life.

Now, as you unpack this, make sure you avoid two traps. The first one is the tendency to compare yourself with other people.

And don't fall into the second trap of blaming others by saying, "It's his/her/their fault I'm this way." There may even be a nugget of truth in that, but you can't change them. Only God, with their cooperation, can make that happen. Besides, this inventory is not about anyone but you. You have to come to grips with and take responsibility for your own stuff. Be fearless.

The Bible says, "If we claim to be without sin, we deceive ourselves and the truth is not in us" (1 John 1:8 NIV). If I can't think of anything to write down, then I'm just living in a world of illusion; the "truth is not in me." If I want to stop killing myself, I've got to stop kidding myself.

This process is about going after deep core character defects like selfishness, pride, envy, insecurity, approval seeking, greed, fear, worry, bitterness, unresolved conflict, and unresolved guilt. Deep stuff. Hidden stuff. God is more than able to bring that out. I know because he's brought them to the surface in me.

It's so helpful to get another person, a trusted friend, involved in this process. And from reading my story, you know that sharing everything I ever did with my sponsor was one of the most, if not the most, powerful steps I took to find freedom. I never thought I would be able to bring that stuff to light with someone else and have them stick around long enough to listen

That's probably why the Bible says, "Confess your sins to each other and pray for each other so that you may be healed" (James 5:16). When I was able to share everything with my sponsor that I'd ever done, it felt like a thousand pounds fell off my shoulders. I actually didn't lose any weight, but it sure felt like it!

We know there is a deep longing within us to come clean and be known. The problem is most of us aren't willing to take the risk of being so transparent. We've been protecting the image thing for so long. There's the fear of rejection, isolation, and embarrassment. And maybe a little self-centered pride still hanging around. So we end up resisting the very thing our hearts have been craving all along.

Dietrich Bonhoeffer wrote, "Many Christians are unthinkably horrified when a 'real sinner' is suddenly discovered among the righteous. So we remain alone with our sin, living in lies and hypocrisy. ... He who is alone with his sins is utterly alone."*

God wants us to do this together; we are all fellow strugglers on a grace journey.

And, of course, as you decide who you can share your inventory list with, choose someone who can keep a confidence, who is not going to gossip or post your secrets on social media. Find a trusted person who understands the value of what you're doing. Confide in someone who is mature enough that they won't be shocked, someone who knows the Lord well enough that they can reflect his grace and wisdom to you. Maybe it's someone who's been exactly where you are, maybe it's a close, trusted friend, or maybe even a Christian counselor.

So, what are you waiting for? Put a bookmark right here and lay this book down for a while. Grab a pen and a notepad and

---

* Dietrich Bonhoeffer, *Life Together: The Classic Exploration of Christian Community* (New York: Harper & Row, 1954), n.p.

invite God to go with you on this journey to the center of the truth. It's easier than "Operation." It won't light up your nose. There'll be no buzzing shocks, and you've got the Great Physician assisting you.

chapter sixteen

MAKE △MENDS

I used to watch the old TV sitcom, *The Andy Griffith Show*. Do you remember that show with good ol' Andy Taylor and Barney, Goober, Floyd, Opie, and Aunt Bee? Maybe you are too young, but when I would watch it, the guy I could relate to the most was Otis. Otis was the self-described "town drunk," and he would stop by the sheriff's office on a regular basis, walk right into a cell, and lock himself in to "sleep it off." The funny thing was that they hung the keys up where he could reach them and leave at any time.

And I resonate with Otis because I have been Otis. Sometimes I have been so comfortable in my cell, that I've forgotten that at any time I could walk out and be free, but that's what this process is all about. The things we've been doing in these steps of embracing our brokenness, being ready to surrender, and evaluating our lives with fearless honesty, are ways that we are choosing to get up and walk out of that cell.

But this one is a tough one. This one is one where I have looked at the comfortable mat in that cell and wanted to walk right back in. See, when you get honest with yourself and take that fearless moral inventory, you find that a lot of the emotion, the pain, the regret, the remorse, the anger, the disappointment, the guilt, and the shame stems from your interaction with—you guessed it—people.

And our responsibility in this step is to do our part to make things right with—you guessed it—people. It's time to make amends or seek forgiveness from those you've hurt, and forgive those who have hurt you.

Neither one of those things are easy. I remember when I made my list. It was complicated. I had to take a couple of road trips. I had to do research. I had to make embarrassing phone calls. I had to stand before people in my shame and wear it, exposed and broken, and ask them to release me from the debt I owed them.

But do you know what was amazing? In those moments, it was like chains were broken. It was like a forest that had been burned to the dirt was now springing up little seeds of life. I started seeing the people who I was making amends to in a whole new way, and it was powerful.

And it's important to point out that this step, making amends and asking for forgiveness, is not about you. It's about you doing whatever your part is to make things right with them. It's about them hearing you own your own stuff, and not about getting anything in return. It is an act of humility, but the reward is great. The reward is getting to let go.

Even if they don't forgive you. Even if you can't make all things right. Even if it doesn't fix the relationship or make everything better. You get to lay down your expectation of that and just choose to do it because it's the right thing to do, and the sheer act of it sets you free.

But there is another kind of amends that is important and powerful, and it's learning to forgive those who have hurt me.

I can't tell you the number of horror stories I've heard from people in my recovery world life. And every one of them, including my own, points to some kind of relational breakdown. Colossians says, "Make allowance for each other's faults, and forgive anyone who offends you. Remember, the Lord forgave you, so you must forgive others" (3:13).

I used to say, "But they owe me! My parents hurt me bad; they owe me! Those kids at school owe me! My brother owes me! That old girlfriend owes me! That ex-spouse owes me! If I let them off the hook, it just wouldn't be fair ... they need to pay!"

Then I read this: "Get rid of all bitterness, rage, anger, harsh words, and slander, as well as all types of evil behavior. Instead, be kind to each other, tenderhearted, forgiving one another, just as God through Christ has forgiven you" (Ephesians 4:31–32).

You see, we owed God. And he didn't give us "fair." He gave us his Son, and he paid the debt that our sins had racked up.

But our human nature rears its ugly head, and we cry out for justice, for retribution. We get an adrenaline rush watching those movies where the really evil guy gets a payback. We are easily deceived into thinking that true release, real freedom, lies in revenge.

But I've learned the hard way that it actually doesn't. It's a lie that our enemy feeds us. And it's a lie that keeps us from getting well.

If you would do a "cost/benefit analysis" of bitterness, you would find enormous cost and zero benefit. It wrecks you physically, emotionally, and spiritually. The Bible talks about how it blinds us to the truth, changes our personality, messes with our prayers, and locks us up in prison. No wonder it says in Job that, "Resentment kills a fool, and envy slays the simple" (Job 5:2 NIV).

Have you been there? Man, I have. You're all upset over something, someone who hurt you, and it might have happened ten, twenty, or thirty years ago. They may have forgotten about it or even passed away. But in your anger, you are allowing them to continue to hurt you. Resentment can't change the past, the problem, or the person. It only hurts you.

It's been my experience, and research backs up this assertion, a lot of people are sick or stay sick because of unresolved bitterness in their lives. You see, it's not so much what you eat but what eats you that will kill you.

I've watched way too many people who refuse to let go of the relational scars and wounds. They won't give up their right to get even. They can't let go of the past. And bitterness literally eats them alive: "Some people stay healthy till the day they die; they die happy and at ease, their bodies well-nourished. Others have no happiness at all; they live and die with bitter hearts" (Job 21:23–25 GNT).

That's a lousy way to live and die.

So, how do you do this? How do you extend forgiveness to those who have hurt you, especially if they didn't ask? I think, just like in that third step of a fearless moral inventory, you start by inviting God to be involved. Again, I think you grab a pen and some paper and you write down a prayer that might go something like: "God, I want to thank you for your incredible kindness, patience, and grace toward me. I admit that I haven't shown the same kind of grace toward those who have hurt me; instead, I have held onto my bitterness, my anger, my thirst for revenge, for way too long. So, I'm asking for your help right now. Please bring to mind all the people I need to forgive, so that I can do this right now."

Then start to list the names of people who come to your mind. If a name comes to your mind just write it down. They may or may not need forgiveness from you. They may be a totally innocent party, but their name may lead you to a story that may take you deeper into discovering the real who that needs forgiveness.

A lot of time we hang onto things and punish ourselves for the wrong choices we've made in the past. So, as you're listing names, also make sure you write down "myself" at the bottom of your list.

Next to unresolved bitterness, unresolved guilt can be a weapon of mass destruction. Forgiving yourself is embracing the truth that God, through Jesus, has already forgiven you, and if God forgives you, you can forgive yourself.

As you prepare to do this, let me tell you what I've learned forgiveness is not.

Forgiveness is not forgetting. You really can't forget everything. Hurts leave scars and sometimes even constant daily reminders because of the circumstances in which their actions have placed you. Forgiveness is not saying, "It's no big deal." It was a big deal. It hurt. Don't minimize it or rationalize it.

Forgiveness is not a feeling. Forgiveness is a choice, a decision of your will. You don't wait until you feel like forgiving. It's a decision to surrender to the authority and leadership of God. To do this is a step of obedience. Remember the Lord forgave you, so you must forgive others. And since God requires you to forgive, it is something that you can do. He's not going ask you to do something that he won't help you do.

Don't wait until you feel like forgiving. You will never get there. Forgive from your heart. Just like you asked God to reveal your character defects, allow God to bring to the surface painful memories and then acknowledge how you feel toward those who've hurt you. If the forgiveness doesn't touch the emotional core of your life, it will be incomplete. Too often we are afraid of the pain, so we bury our emotions deep down inside us. Let God bring them out.

You see, forgiveness is God's way of ending the cycle of abuse. And right now you might be saying, "But Keith, you don't know how much they hurt me!" You're right, I don't. But I do know that until you let go of your anger and hatred, that person is allowed to keep hurting you. We can't hit rewind and undo the past, but we can be free from it.

Again, I'm learning new stuff from the Bible every day of my life, like this one, "Never pay back evil with more evil. Do things in such a way that everyone can see you are honorable. Do all that you can to live in peace with everyone. Dear friends, never take revenge. Leave that to the righteous anger of God. For the Scriptures say, 'I will take revenge; I will pay them back,' says the Lord" (Romans 12:17–19).

You need to give up your right to get even and let God deal with them. And don't wait for the person to ask for your forgiveness; there's a little pride thing going on with that. You make the first move. Jesus, who was completely innocent, modeled that on the cross when he said, "Father, forgive them. They do not know what they are doing" (Luke 23:34 NLV).

I have learned also that I need to forgive often. Memories come back. You run into people from time to time. You might have to deal with an ex-spouse, and it brings back old feelings every time you let your kids get into the car with them. In that moment you forgive again.

Compile your list and as you get to that first person, make the choice to forgive him or her for every painful memory that comes to your mind. You focus on that person until you are sure you have dealt with all the remembered pain. Release them to God and start working your way down the list.

And don't say, *God, help me forgive.* He is already helping you in this process. Don't say, *God, I want to forgive.* You say, *God, I choose to forgive* _____ *for what they have done or failed to do, which made me feel* _____. *I choose not to hold on to this resentment anymore. Thanks for setting me free from the bondage of my bitterness. I give up my right to get even and ask you to heal my damaged emotions.*

Make amends. Choose forgiveness and walk out of the prison of bitterness. The keys are hanging up right outside your cell.

chapter seventeen

THINK A WHOLE
NEW WAY

There was a song about fifteen years ago by the pop/rock group Sister Hazel, where the lyrics rang out: "If you want to be somebody else; If you're tired of fighting battles with yourself; ... Change your mind."

They were right. I'm learning that the real challenge to you and me being all that God wants us to be lies between our ears.

Jesus told us that we have an enemy and even called him "the father of lies" (John 8:44 NLV). And that enemy wants to keep us locked up with guilt, shame, and worthlessness. He loves to see us wrestle with a tortured soul; the last thing he wants for you and me is freedom. He targets the mind, and he knows that if he can get us to believe his lies, instead of God's truth, he can keep us stuck.

You see, if you can influence thinking, you can influence behavior. Because the way we behave is always a reflection of the way we think. The Bible says, "For as [a man] thinks in his heart, so is he" (Proverbs 23:7 NLV). Which just means that what makes you and me the way we are is the way we think. You see, the battlefield is not so much our behavior as it is our mind.

Paul says, "Don't copy the behavior and customs of this world, but let God transform you into a new person by changing the way you think. Then you will learn to know God's will for you, which is good and pleasing and perfect" (Romans 12:2).

It took me a couple times of reading this to understand, but it's really important to see that there are actually two parts to this process of living a new way: God's part and our part.

God's part is the transformation. Paul is saying that you have to let a power that is greater than you go to work on you because only he has the power to change you and me from the inside out. A friend told me that the Greek word used for "transform" in that Scripture is *metamorpho*. That word sound familiar? It's where the word *metamorphosis* comes from, and I like that picture because a caterpillar can't change himself into a butterfly on his own strength and power. Its job is to surrender to the process of change. That's the way it is with us too. Transformation is God's part.

But my part and your part in this transformation is changing the way we think. We have to renew our mind to a whole new way of thinking. My friend told me, "You can't solve a problem with the same mind that created it!" You've got to change your mind.

There are two words that have helped me do this: *feed* and *focus*. What you feed your mind will determine the release of your full potential. I've been trying to eat healthier. I've been working out and being more selective about what I put in my body. I've fed my body a lot of bad stuff, a lot of junk food through the years. But it's nothing compared to the junk with which I used to feed my mind.

If I am feeding my mind pornographic images, it does something to the way I view other people, and the way I see relationships.

If I'm always thumbing through magazines looking at celebrities and those perfect bodies who live rich and famous lifestyles, it messes with my contentment factor, makes me insecure in my own skin, and skews my perspective on the importance of stuff.

If I am feeding my mind with all the political nastiness on social media, it turns me into a cynical, joyless, and even hate-filled person.

I'm learning that whether it's movies, books, music, conversations, or jokes, I have to be careful what I am constantly feeding my mind. My mind and your mind will be shaped by what we feed it.

One of the significant Scriptures that has practically helped shape my thinking says, "whatever is true, whatever is noble, whatever is right, whatever is pure, whatever is lovely, whatever is admirable—if anything is excellent or praiseworthy—think about such things" (Philippians 4:8 NIV).

I like to think of that as kind of a "truth grid" to drop my thoughts through and as I do, it's pretty amazing the way the Holy Spirit will help me filter those thoughts in the moment.

For instance, you might say in your mind, *God, you said whatever is lovely, and that girl on the cover of the swimsuit issue sure is lovely!* And the Holy Spirit responds, *Yeah, that may be true, but your thoughts are not pure. That's not the right thing to feed your mind. The way that makes you devalue women is not admirable.*

Or you think, *God, you said think about whatever is true, and what they are saying in the breakroom about my boss right now is absolutely true. He is a jerk! And I want to pile on and add my opinion.* But the Holy Spirit says, *You know, what they are saying might be true, but you fueling the negativity is not noble. That is not being an excellent employee. Your motives certainly aren't praiseworthy. You need to walk away.*

See how having that internal truth grid helps?

Reading the Bible has helped me renew my mind like nothing else. As I've been feeding my mind on God's truth, I've been growing and God is producing some pretty cool fruit in my life. I'm learning that it is alive and life-changing. You really ought to try it.

The reason to read the Bible is not to get extra credit from God or to gain more knowledge so you can win in a game of Bible Jeopardy. It's to plant yourself by the life-giving river so your life can produce fruit. Psalm 1 says, "But they delight in the law of the LORD, meditating on it day and night. They are like trees planted along the riverbank, bearing fruit each season. Their leaves never wither, and they prosper in all they do" (vv. 2–3).

The job of the tree is not to produce fruit. Its job is to be planted by the river.

That's why Paul writes, "Let your roots grow down into him, and let your lives be built on him. Then your faith will grow strong in the truth you were taught, and you will overflow with thankfulness" (Colossians 2:7).

One of the practical ways I've learned to let my roots go down deep is to meditate on God's truth. It's a value in my twelve-step program and throughout God's Word. When I say meditate I'm not talking about lighting some incense, getting in an awkward position, and humming. No, the old adage is, "If you can worry, you can meditate." It's just turning a thought over and over in your mind. As you do that, your mind is being fed much-needed truth and you develop new patterns of thinking. I've learned that you can't think a bad thought and a good thought at the same time. One of them has to go, so replacing that negative thought with a new one begins to change the way you think.

For example, you might read, "Cast all your anxiety on him because he cares for you" (1 Peter 5:7 NIV). So, when you start feeling anxious, instead of filling your mind with what might happen, could happen, or should happen, you start a new thought churning: *I have to cast this off … I need to give this to God … why do I carry this around?* And you just turn it over and over in your mind.

This is a big deal because life gets hard, and when it does, you can bet the enemy will be there to clutter your mind saying, *See, God doesn't love you; your whole life is falling apart. You'll never change; you ought to worry. You need to be anxious; God doesn't care about you.* But when you have been feeding your mind the truth, you are able to stay rooted by the riverbank and recognize those lies for what they are.

At the same time, what you choose to focus on has your attention, and what has your attention has you.

It's like a golfer who steps up on the tee box and notices that there is water on the right. So in his mind he begins to think, *Oh man, there's water on the right. There's water on the right. There's water on the right.* Where do you think he's going to hit it? In the water on the right!

When you take your motorcycle license test, you have to swerve through orange cones. The key to passing the test? Don't focus on the cones, but focus on the space between. Whatever has your focus, has you.

Sometimes we say, *Okay, then I'm not going to think about that. I'm not going to think about that. I'm not going to think about that.* And while you are telling yourself to not think about that, what are you doing? Yeah, thinking about that!

So, it's not so much to resist, as it is to replace. You have to change your focus. And our mind has that ability to change focus.

In your mind, throughout the day, you really can choose to move toward gratitude, or you can choose to move toward entitlement. You can set your mind on joy and contentment or set it on dissatisfaction and envy. You can choose your focus.

Colossians 3 tells us that, "Since, then, you have been raised with Christ, set your hearts on things above, where Christ is, seated at the right hand of God. Set your minds on things above, not on earthly things" (vv. 1–2 NIV). We can actually place our minds where we want to put them.

Let me tell you from my own experience. When you set your mind on yourself and when your focus is on earthly things, worldly stuff, chasing bling, popularity, and fame, the inevitable result is worry, anxiety, guilt, envy, greed, unhealthy competition, pride, lust, insecurity, fear, and discouragement.

But when you "set your mind on things above" and when Jesus is your focus and you choose to move through your day with an others-centered focus like he did, then all that other junk gets replaced by hope, confidence, humility, love, laughter, patience, security, and unexplainable peace. It's like Isaiah 26:3 says, "You will keep in perfect peace all who trust in you, all whose thoughts are fixed on you!"

It all comes down to your focus.

So, every day you roll out of bed and say, *God, today I again surrender my life to you. Keep me focused on your presence in my life today, all day. Help me listen well as you try to guard my reactions, my tone, my attitude, and my choices. May my thoughts be fixed on you.*

This is a big deal for many of us because we spent so many years with our minds fixed on everything but God, right?

Remember God will transform. We have to change the way we think.

My friend told me once about his brother-in-law's farm in Kentucky. He said that there was a path going from the barn to his main field. He could drive his tractor out of the barn, put it on that path, take his hands completely off the steering wheel, and it would go down that path and perfectly through the gate into the field. He said the reason his tractor could do that is because he had been up and down that path so many times that there were deep ruts in that road. All he had to do was get the tires aligned with the ruts, and it would automatically do its thing.

Then my friend told me, "Keith, you've been driving in the same old ruts for thirty years; you need new ruts. You need new pathways, new patterns of thinking, new ways of coping, and new ways of reacting. You have to change your focus. Just feed and focus, feed and focus, and feed and focus."

So I'm learning that as you feed and focus, your way of thinking begins to change. And as your way of thinking begins to change, your way of behaving starts to change. And as your behavior starts to change, old habits start to die. And as old habits start to die, freedom starts to define your life, and real lasting inside out transformation starts to overwhelm you!

So, let God *metamorpho* you into a new creation by changing the way you think.

chapter eighteen

ENCOURAGE OTHERS WITH MY LIFE AND STORY

That plaque of my disabled placard nailed to a cross is still hanging in my garage, and every time I see it, I smile. I'm reminded of how I've been healed and set free, and how I've been told to "Take up my mat and walk!"

I am so grateful that Jesus didn't say, "Throw that nasty mat away, and walk." I'm so grateful for the mat I have been charged to carry so that I can tell my story of how amazing grace saved a wretch like me.

The final step in my recovery program reads like this: "Having experienced a spiritual awakening, I must now step outside of myself and encourage others with my story and continually changing life."

I borrowed the term, "spiritual awakening" from the twelve-step program I'm a part of (I've borrowed most of the phrases and truths I say these days from the *Big Book* of AA and the Big

Book of Jesus), but I wanted to use that term because what I have undergone is not a mere "religious experience;" it is so much more!

It's having your eyes opened and coming face to face with the reality of your life. It's dropping the denial. It's coming out of the dark and seeing the light. It's pushing off the bottom and reaching up for God's help. It's breaking through the surface. It's coming up to breathe!

When you have that spiritual awakening—when you are experiencing a transformation from the inside out that you never dreamed possible—it's hard to keep that quiet.

Whether it's getting asked to the prom, making the team, receiving an engagement ring, a scholarship offer, a big job promotion, or the results of a pregnancy test, some things are just about impossible to keep quiet.

It's hard to contain the fact that you have been touched by amazing grace. When you've been set free like I have, you can't help but walk with a different spring in your step. All that weight, all that baggage, and all that poison is gone. It feels really, really good to be walking free. And there's nothing quite as powerful as a freedom story.

So hear God say to you today, *Take up your mat and walk!* He wants to use your story. He wants to use your life. I like to say that I think that God wants us to be environmentally conscientious and take care of this planet, and there are lots of ways we are discovering to do that, whether it's lower emissions from cars, alternate fuel sources, or energy efficient light bulbs. And I believe that God sets the example by the way he's always been into recycling.

In fact, God is consumed with recycling. Now while it's true he does love the planet, he loves the people on it a million times more. And what he will do, if we'll let him, is to take all the garbage from our lives—all the nasty, smelly trash and all the toxic waste—and recycle it into something good.

Like those creative people who go to flea markets, garage sales, and the scratch and dent section of furniture stores and turn broken and scarred junk into something incredible, God is really, really good at making the old into new, the wasted into purpose, and the dead alive. He can recycle the pain and garbage in your life into an incredible story that could help someone else's life.

You see, God not only wants to save you, forgive you, heal you, restore you, change you, and guide you … he wants *to use* you.

We all have amazing worth in God's eyes. He created us, breathed life into us, and he put within every one of us a unique personality and unique gifts, so that we can make a difference in this world. Even though we can make a royal mess of our lives, if we will humble ourselves and let him go to work, God will recycle all that nasty stuff for good. No one is worthless. No one is useless. He wants you to take up your mat and walk. He wants to use your healed life to help other people.

Having experienced a spiritual awakening, I must now step outside of myself and encourage others with my story and continually changing life.

I used the phrase "continually changing life" because you don't have to wait until you are completely there to be used by God. Let God use you as a person in process.

You may be like me and not have a ton of great insight. You may not yet be able to offer the kind of counsel and wisdom as someone who's further down the road than you. But you can say to people, "I'm not where I want to be, but I'm not where I used to be. God is changing me. He's setting my feet on a new path, and helping me walk a new direction."

You know, there's always a "so that" involved in transformation. Companies will make changes in their business, "so that ... ." Teams will make changes in line-ups, personnel, or coaching staffs "so that ... ." There is always a goal in mind. God does the same when he changes someone. Check this out: "God saved you by his grace when you believed. And you can't take credit for this; it is a gift from God. Salvation is not a reward for the good things we have done, so none of us can boast about it. For we are God's masterpiece. He has created us anew in Christ Jesus, so we can do the good things he planned for us long ago" (Ephesians 2:8–10).

You see, God planned to use my life and yours all along. But you maybe took a detour like me and did your own thing, but by his grace and power he brought you back. And you can't brag about that because he did it. And he did it *so that* he could use your life to do the good things he'd always dreamed you would do.

I never imagined I would get to do something like this. Me write a book? A former alcoholic, drug addict who was addicted to and distributed porn? I think all the time, *Who am I to get to do this?* I am so grateful. I'm sure there are people in my past who are absolutely shocked that I'm doing this with my life, but not as shocked as I am.

I'm telling you, from personal experience, if you will cooperate with the leadership of God, he can and will recycle all of your pain, your failures, your screw-ups, your dirty secrets, and your past into an unexpected ministry to help other people.

When you become broken, humble, dependent upon God, grateful for grace, and grateful for a second chance in life, then you become a real player in God's redemptive plan.

You become empathetic, compassionate, and understanding, because you've been there. You know you've been forgiven much, so like Jesus said, now you are able to love much. You know how futile self-help is. You know how destructive bitterness is. You know how freeing forgiveness is. You understand the value of complete honesty. You know where to access real transformational power. You know what it takes to make the courageous choice to walk down a different path. You understand the power of feeding your mind and changing your focus. You are in the process of changing a little more every day, one day at a time. And every day you start by saying, *Today I'm going to act justly, love mercifully, and walk humbly with you, God.*

I mean, think about it, if you were God, isn't that the type of person you'd want on your team? That's the kind of person I would want working for me. Second Corinthians 5:17–18 says:

This means that anyone who belongs to Christ has become a new person. The old life is gone; a new life has begun! And all of this is a gift from God, who brought us back to himself through Christ. And God has given us this task of reconciling people to him. For God was in Christ, reconciling the world to himself, no longer counting people's sins against them. And he gave us this wonderful message of reconciliation.

God uses you and me to carry the message of hope, to be his representative and his ambassador, to tell the story of how God woke us up, pulled us out, and set us free.

Check out another one of those "so that" Scriptures: "He comforts us in all our troubles so that we can comfort others. When they are troubled, we will be able to give them the same comfort God has given us" (2 Corinthians 1:4).

I'm blown away by how many people God puts in my path that need the same kind of touch from him that I have received.

You never know how God will use you. You never know when your story, no matter what it is, will intersect someone else's life and give them hope.

Sometimes we think that God only uses perfect people, really gifted people, or the spiritually elite. That's just not true. God has always used ordinary people, broken people.

Please don't misunderstand, people are helped immensely when we share from our strengths, but many more are helped when we're also not afraid to be honest about our weaknesses, and the way that God is giving us the power to change.

Who better to help someone struggling with alcohol or drug addiction than someone who's been there? Who better to help someone with an eating disorder than someone who's been there? Who better to help someone through the pain of abuse, unfaithfulness, bankruptcy, the loss of a child, a miscarriage, or chemotherapy than someone who's been there?

There is no more effective healer than a wounded healer: someone who's been there. God never wastes a hurt! Never. If you are willing, he will take your pain and struggle and recycle it in such a way that your life will ripple on people in ways you never dreamed.

Take up your mat and walk!

Pray that God will intersect your life with other people. And then notice them. Never see them as an interruption, but as an answer to your prayer to help someone else. Seize the opportunity to humbly, tactfully, and graciously share what life is like now that you and God are walking this new road together. All you have to be able to say to help somebody else is, "The road is long, but with God's help I'm getting there one step at a time. And I'd sure love to take you along with me, how about it?"

And as you share your story and as you encourage and mentor and coach and sponsor other people who are where you used to be, pretty soon you will feel as impassioned as Paul felt when he wrote in Acts, "What matters most to me is to finish what God started: the job the Master Jesus gave me of letting everyone I meet know all about this incredibly extravagant generosity of God" (20:24 MSG).

And that's exactly how I feel these days. I've spent a lot of time telling you my story. You know that I am a man who is recovering from materialism, lust, jealousy, resentment, gluttony, procrastination, lying, anger, inferiority, grief, heartbreak, gossip, malice, et cetera.

But you also need to know that I am a man who has experienced the grace, patience, power, and unfailing love of Jesus Christ in his life. He gave me a new start. He took out my cold, hard heart and gave me a new soft one. He took me from hard core to soft serve, literally and metaphorically. He gave me a new direction to walk and some new shoes to wear. He surrounded me with people to help me along the way. He is transforming me daily with the same power that raised Jesus from the dead. So as long as there is breath in my lungs, you will not get me to shut up about the kindness of God. It's part of my recovery, and it's part of yours.

Now's the time. Want to get well? Surrender, get honest, make amends, and start thinking a whole new way, and as soon you're done? Grab someone who needs the hope you've found, and *take up your mat and walk.*

ABOUT
THE AUTHORS

Keith Repult was the owner of the second largest porn distribution company in the country and one of the top ten manufacturing companies in the world, living a life of addiction, hiding, and hurting. After giving his life over to the leadership of Christ, selling his companies, and working a twelve-step program, Keith has become a new man—a man who has traded wealth for wholeness, addiction for acceptance, and prestige for peace. Now the Recovery Pastor at Mission Church in Ventura, California, Keith tells his story whenever he can to whomever will listen to remind each of us that you've never gone too far and you're never in too deep to be made new by the grace of God. Keith lives in Ventura with his son, two daughters, and beautiful wife, Samantha, and together they own Surf 'n Yogurt. For more, go to keithrepult.com.

Jen Oakes has been writing since her mom gave her a pen and a journal when she was a little girl and made her sit in her room for an hour of "quiet time" every day. And now that she's a mom, she realizes that her mom was a genius—not just for the whole "send your kid to their room for a quiet time" thing, but also because it developed in Jen a deep love for writing. She considers it one of the greatest privileges of her life to be a part of watching and telling stories of individuals who have been redeemed by the grace of God. Jen is passionate about coffee, listening to vinyl records, open windows, reading, writing, hiking, being outside, and people. She currently serves on staff at Mission Church in Ventura, California, and is happily married to her favorite person, T. D. Oakes. Together they have two incredible kids.

Mike Breaux is a nationally known communicator and has served as a pastor for Canyon Ridge Christian Church in Las Vegas, Nevada, Southland Christian Church in Lexington, Kentucky, Willow Creek Community Church and Heartland Community Church in the Chicago area. Mike is currently the teaching pastor for three churches in Southern California: Real Life Church in Valencia, Eastside Christian Church in Anaheim, and Christ's Church of the Valley in San Dimas. He is the author of *Making Ripples* and *Identity Theft*. While Mike has had an incredible impact in ministry all over the country, his greatest desire is to simply live a life that acts justly, loves mercy, and walks humbly with God. Mike and his wife, Debbie, have three children and nine grandchildren.

Keith (center) preparing for water baptism

RESOURCES

Along with our book *Just Breathe*, we recommend the following resources as aids for you in your search for healing and wholeness.

A Hunger for Healing: The Twelve Steps as a Classic Model for Christian Spiritual Growth, by Keith Miller

Alcoholics Anonymous: The Big Book

Celebrate Recovery, by Rick Warren and John Baker

Maximum Faith: Live Like Jesus, by George Barna

Embracing Brokenness, by Alan E. Nelson

The Me I Want to Be: Becoming God's Best Version of You, by John Ortberg

Freeway: A Not-So-Perfect Guide to Freedom, by Mike Foster

People of the Second Chance: A Guide to Bringing Life-Saving Love to the World, by Mike Foster

Open: What Happens When You Get Real, Get Honest, and Get Accountable, by Craig Gross

Pure Eyes: A Man's Guide to Sexual Integrity, by Craig Gross and Steven Luff

When You, Then God: Seven Things God Is Waiting to Do in Your Life, by Rusty George

Life on Mission: God's People Finding God's Heart for the World, by Tim Harlow

Identity Theft: Reclaiming Who God Created You to Be, by Mike Breaux